Later Chinese
Bronzes

Rose Kerr

Later Chinese Bronzes

Photography by Ian Thomas

Bamboo Publishing Ltd in association with
the Victoria and Albert Museum

Victoria and Albert Museum · Far Eastern Series

Published 1990 by Bamboo Publishing Ltd,
719 Fulham Road, London SW6 5UL, in
association with the Victorian and Albert
Museum.

British Library Cataloguing in Publication Data
Kerr, Rose, *1953*–
 Later Chinese bronzes. – (Far Eastern series).
 1. Chinese bronzes.
 I. Title II. Victoria and Albert Museum III. Series
 739'.512'0931

ISBN 1-870076-11-7

K8

Designed by Denyer Design Associates
Typeset in England by P4 Graphics Ltd
Printed in Singapore by Toppan Printing Co. Ltd

Contents

Chronological Table

Neolithic period	about 5000–about 1700 BC
Bronze age	about 1700 BC–AD 220
(Xia dynasty	historical identity unproven)
Shang dynasty	about 1700–1027 BC
Zhou dynasty	1027–221 BC
Qin dynasty	221–207 BC
Han dynasty	206 BC–AD 220
Six dynasties period	220–580
Sui dynasty	581–618
Tang dynasty	618–906
Liao dynasty	907–1125
Five dynasties	907–960
Song dynasty	960–1279
Northern Song dynasty	960–1127
Southern Song dynasty	1128–1279
Jin dynasty	1115–1234
Yuan dynasty	1280–1368
Ming dynasty	1368–1644
Qing dynasty	1644–1911

Ming Dynasty Reign Periods

Hongwu	1368-1398
Jianwen	1399-1402
Yongle	1403-1424
Hongxi	1425
Xuande	1426-1435
Zhengtong	1436-1449
Jingtai	1450-1456
Tianshun	1457-1464
Chenghua	1465-1487
Hongzhi	1488-1505
Zhengde	1506-1521
Jiajing	1522-1566
Longqing	1567-1572
Wanli	1573-1620
Taichang	1620
Tianqi	1621-1627
Chongzhen	1628-1644

Qing Dynasty Reign Periods

Shunzhi	1644-1661
Kangxi	1662-1722
Yongzheng	1723-1735
Qianlong	1736-1795
Jiaqing	1796-1820
Daoguang	1821-1850
Xianfeng	1851-1861
Tongzhi	1862-1874
Guangxu	1875-1908
Xuantong	1909-1911

Note on Spelling and Pronunciation

The *pinyin* system of romanising Chinese script is used throughout, following the spelling given in *Xinhua zidian,* revised edition (Peking, 1971). The only exceptions are Chinese terms and proper names within quotations, which are left in their original form, and the place names Peking, Canton, Nanking and Taipei. Since no agreed standard exists governing word division in romanised Chinese, the grouping of characters has been left to individual authors to carry out as seems appropriate in individual cases.

The following few hints may help the reader unfamiliar with the system at least to pronounce words to themselves:
Initial *zh-,* as English *j-*
Initial *x-,* as English *s-*
Initial *c-,* as English *ts-*
Initial *q-,* as English *ch-*

Introduction

This book is called *Later Chinese Bronzes*, a title which should be explained. The 'later' is used to encompass pieces made during the Song, Yuan, Ming and Qing dynasties, a period of some nine hundred years between about 1000 and 1900 AD. Bronzes from this broad timespan are grouped together under the simple generic term 'later' in order to distinguish them from examples made during China's first great bronze age. Bronze was initially cast in China around 1700 BC, and the bronze age is usually defined as ending with the Han dynasty in 220 AD, by which time other metals were already in use. The splendour and technical excellence of these early pieces has made them a prime field for study. When research into Chinese bronzes is undertaken, it is almost always concerned with 'early' examples.

The production of bronze in China, however, did not end with the Han dynasty. Figures and vessels continued to be made for tombs and for temple altars, and to serve in the home as wash basins, incense burners, vases and ewers. In the absence of glass, polished metal was employed as a reflector, and bronze mirrors continued in use until the present century. The rise of the pottery industry led to the substitution of high-fired ceramics for metal in both religious and secular contexts. Porcelain was cheaper and easier to replace than metal. Thus the history of bronze working in the last few centuries of China's history is a varied and fragmentary one, covering a wide range of usages.

Several short pieces of research have been undertaken in the field of later bronze, and a list of some of these publications is included in the bibliography and in the notes. It will be seen that a number of them refer to bronze vessels in the Victoria and Albert Museum's collection. The reason for this is the extraordinary richness of the Museum's holdings. The Far Eastern Department has more than two thousand examples of later Chinese and Japanese bronze in its collection. Many were acquired in the period 1860 to 1910, when the Museum was still collecting groups of Asian artefacts in large quantities. More than 150 bronzes were purchased on one occasion from the shop of a Parisian dealer who specialised in Japanese crafts to satisfy the current European fashion for 'Japonaiserie'. All of his goods were believed to be Japanese, until later research proved that some were in fact Chinese. The importing to Japan of Chinese bronzes for use in the tea ceremony and for flower arranging had led to their preservation there. Yet other vessels were bought in China itself; some have a provenance, but many more do not.

It is obvious that a single institution's collection cannot provide information on all aspects of such a complex subject. Nonetheless, I hope that this book will address some of the issues involved and will stimulate further research.

With certain exceptions, the problem of dating later bronzes is acute. While the age of an object is not necessarily its most important attribute, it is a significant factor when trying to distinguish large groups of similar vessels, e.g. incense burners with the reign mark of Xuande (1426-35). There are a number of these censers in the collection (p. 35).

In order to gain a more complete picture of the development of bronze styles than simple visual examination and evaluation can provide, the subject has been approached from several angles. The first approach involves evidence derived from textual sources, and the second comparative material provided by archaeological excavation and objects in other more easily datable media such as ceramics. The third approach, a scientific one, has been extensively utilised in the study of archaic bronze vessels. However, as yet there has been hardly any analytical work done on later bronzes.

With the aid of a generous grant from the Virginia and Edward Chow Foundation, the Victoria and Albert Museum (V&A) was able to engage the services of Maria Fabrizi, who worked for six months on studying components analysis, patination and gilding. The results of her research are included in the text, and they provide new and invaluable data for the understanding of later Chinese bronzes.[1]

The metal analyses were carried out using non-destructive and non-intrusive energy dispersive X-ray energy fluorescence analysis (EDXRF). The choice of X-ray fluorescence analysis as the main investigative technique was taken to enable a large group of objects to be surveyed in a short time. Comparisons could be made between groups of objects, and between parts in multi-component objects, and trends discerned. The policy of the Museum is to preserve the integrity of the objects and therefore sampling must be kept to a minimum. The technique which satisfies this criterion, and which is available in the Conservation Department of the Victoria and Albert Museum, is EDXRF. The EDXRF used in the study was a Tracor 'Dubois' 404 Object Analyzer fitted with a molybdenum target X-ray tube operated at 49 kV and 0.20 mA with an air path.

Organic materials were identified, using a Perkin-Elmer 1700 Infrared Fourier Transform Spectrometer. Diffuse reflectance methods were adopted and only very tiny samples were required.

These methods did not cause any damage to the pieces analysed, but had the disadvantage of lost precision where no sample preparation could be carried out. We hope that our preliminary explorative analyses will lead to further detailed work in the future. Many problems still await examination.

Two pieces were later sampled for analysis at the Research Laboratory for Archaeology at Oxford using thermoluminescence dating analysis. The pieces thus treated were those which proved exceptionally difficult to identify by any other means. Small samples were taken from core material in hollow interstices of the vessels so that the bronze bodies themselves were undamaged.

In connection with the scientific analyses described above I should like to thank the Chow Foundation in Geneva for their financial support and Maria Fabrizi who undertook so thorough a study of the bronzes in so short a period. Thanks are also due to Graham Martin, Head of the Science Section at the V&A, to David Scouller and Gretchen Shearer who worked at the V&A, and to Doreen Stoneham at Oxford.

The preparation of the text has been greatly aided by all members of the Far Eastern Department, both in practical ways and by comments on the manuscript. Louise Hofman coordinated the photographic programme and Ian Thomas took the excellent photographs.

I should also like to thank Pamela Vandiver, Jessica Rawson, Chang Lin-sheng, and Helen Wang who searched the archaeological literature for me.

Sources for the Study of Chinese Bronzes

A survey of the whole field of Chinese literature relating to Chinese bronzes is beyond the capacity of this author, and would in any case have little place in such a book. The scale of published works is large; a book published in 1933 called *San dai Qin Han jin wen zhu lu biao* ('Bibliography of Works Dealing With Inscriptions On Bronzes of the Xia, Shang, Zhou, Qin and Han Dynasties') by Luo Fuyi, calculated that thirty-five treatises encompassing 5,780 bronzes had been published since about AD 1000. As this tally was mainly composed of pieces with inscriptions, a huge total number of bronzes must be envisaged.[2] The purpose of this chapter is to indicate some categories of literature which might aid the study of bronzes, and to cite certain helpful examples from among their ranks.

Many ancient bronzes had inscriptions which gave information about provenance, ownership and function. The inscriptions were cast into the metal using characters which bore a resemblance to those still in use today. In fact, trained historians can read archaic bronze script without much difficulty. In addition to facts provided by the bronzes themselves, there are also extant written works. Most of these are histories, like the *Shang shu* ('Book of Historical Documents') which includes some authentic passages completed before the Han dynasty (206 BC–AD 220). Another semi-fictional history is the *Zuo zhuan* ('Zuo Commentary'), dating to the period 350–180 BC. Then there is the *Zhu shu ji nian* ('Annals on Bamboo Strips'), which tradition states was compiled around 300 BC.[3] These books mention the casting and presentation of vessels. However, they also refer to happenings which are corroborated by bronze inscriptions. In many cases the artefacts describe events in greater detail or from a different standpoint, and thus actually substantiate the histories.[4]

By the period with which this study begins, the Song dynasty (960–1279), a larger body of textual information exists. Various forms of history book, like the 'annalistic histories' (*bian nian*) and 'miscellaneous histories' (*za shi*), deal with persons and events in a rather indiscriminate fashion. However, as Song bronzes do not tend to bear long descriptive commentaries, these works are not very helpful for comparative purposes. More useful are the geographies, particularly those dealing with specific regions and towns. Good examples of the *genre* will contain details of surrounding scenery, official personnel, important buildings and ancient remains. They may have a section on 'miscellanea' that can include archaeological clues. Records were updated at intervals, so that there are often two or three editions concerning the same place, written during the Song and succeeding dynasties.[5] The local geographies for the Zhenjiang region were of use in investigating the provenance of the vase in Plates 31, 32, 46 and 47.

Another body of literature is that comprised by epigraphers' catalogues. During the Song period a growing interest in the past led a number of scholars to collect ancient bronzes. Their curiosity was no doubt fed by the excavation of ancient sites. Such discoveries were not new; peasants had been digging up treasures in the course of farming for hundreds of years. But now each fresh find was sure of a ready market. Rich men, antiquarians and government ministers competed for these material manifestations of China's long and unbroken civilisation. The Emperor Huizong (reigned 1101-26) is said to have built up a collection of ten thousand pieces. This interest in ancient bronzes inevitably led to tomb plundering and to forgery. One of many problems in the study of later metalwork is the identification of Song copies and their differentiation from fakes of Ming and Qing date.

When good bronze collections had been formed, proud owners sought to publish them. This was sometimes done through the medium of illustrated catalogues. Although an outline drawing accompanied the description of each piece, the main thrust of research was directed towards the deciphering and reproduction of bronze inscriptions. This epigraphical approach to the subject was peculiar to China, whose written language had such close connections with all branches of the arts. It was an approach adopted by most subsequent catalogue compilers. Indeed, many contemporary researchers, both Chinese and Western, make epigraphy the basis of their study.

Among the many catalogues published, six have been selected for brief survey.[6] The earliest extant work, and the most thorough, is a book called *Kao gu tu* ('Researches on Archaeology with Drawings'), compiled in 1092 by a man called Lu Dalin. Mr Lu had examined 211 vessels, some in the palace, and others from more than thirty private collections. He reproduced a rubbing and decipherment of the inscription on each piece, together with its shape, size and weight. He noted exactly where each piece was bought and by whom, as well as the name of the place where it had been unearthed (if appropriate) and the circumstances under which it had been found. He further set up a system for the classification of bronzes by period, which was used by most post-Song compilers. Thus the work adopted an investigative approach and was in its time the closest thing to an archaeological report. An increased number of pieces for study led to the compilation of a shorter supplementary volume, published about seventy or eighty years later. This book was called the *Xu kao gu tu* ('Continuation of the "Researches on Archaeology with Drawings"'), and was possibly based on notes by Lu Dalin but completed by some other anonymous scholar.

The *Chong xiu Xuanhe bo gu tu lu* ('Drawings and Lists of All the Antiques Known at the Xuanhe Period. Revised Edition') is often known by its abbreviated title *Bo gu tu lu* ('Drawings and Lists of Antiques'). Although it has rather confused origins,[7] the work claims to have been finished in 1123. It catalogues the forms and inscriptions of the 840-odd bronzes which were in the palace collection at the Xuanhe period (1119-23). For this reason, and unlike the *Kao gu tu,* it included pieces without inscriptions. The compilers used the same system as the earlier book for describing bronzes and assigning them to different periods. It was more

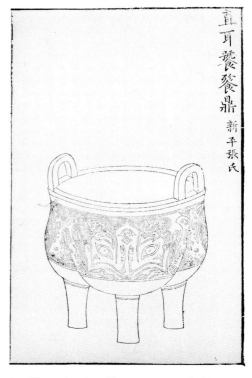

2 *Illustration from Kao gu tu,* compiled in 1092. This edition 1601, *juan* 1, p. 17.

Opposite page:
1 *Bronze vase,* Song-Yuan dynasty, 12th–14th century, height 15.5 cm, 5384-1901.

14

accurate as far as the names of forms and the functions of vessels were concerned, for it corrected several mistakes made in the *Kao gu tu*. It also went some way towards defining bronze decorations, and many of its descriptive terms are still in use today. However, because the book insisted that all palace pieces were made during the Shang, Zhou or Han periods (i.e. prior to AD 220), and that none of them could be later imitations, its practical use is limited, as other Song scholars noted at the time.[8]

Jin shi lu ('Collection of Texts on Bronze and Stone') was compiled by Zhao Mingcheng and his wife the eminent poetess Li Qingzhao, and published between 1119 and 1125. It is divided into ten chapters and tables, some two thousand rubbings of inscriptions, with added explanations of when the pieces were made, and other relevant details. In the preface, Zhao tackles the problem of discrepancies between transmitted history and excavated evidence. His is a modern approach, preferring practical proofs:

> When archaeological materials are used to examine these things, thirty to forty per cent of the data is in conflict. That is because historical writings are produced by latter-day writers and cannot fail to contain errors. But the inscriptions on stone and bronze are made at the time the events take place and can be trusted without reservation . . .[9]

In a touching postscript Li Qingzhao explained that she was writing as a widow in straitened circumstances, in order that the couple's joint work should be completed. Li and Zhao, who lived and studied in the Northern Song capital of Kaifeng, were so short of money that they had to resort to pawning clothes in order to collect the

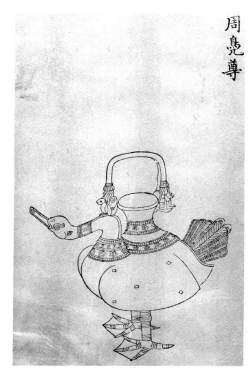

3 *Illustration from Bo gu tu lu*, compiled around 1123. This edition 1588, *juan* 7, p. 10. Courtesy of the Percival David Foundation of Chinese Art.

Opposite page:

4 *Pouring vessel in form of a goose,* bronze inlaid with gold and silver and copying an ancient vessel. Song dynasty (960–1279), height 16.5 cm, Salting Bequest, M.731-1910.

Left:

5 *Base of vessel in Plate 4* showing flakes of malachite, stuck on as part of artificial patination.

precious rubbings. They completed their study through heroic effort only to suffer disaster when a large part of the collection was lost. Zhao then died, but thanks to his wife's devotion their great work has been preserved.[10]

Another unremarkable work is the *Xiao tang ji gu lu* ('Records of the Collection of Antiques of the Whistling Studio') of Wang Qiu. It was probably written soon after 1123, just before conquering northerners defeated the Song armies and forced the court to flee south from Kaifeng. The invaders founded the Jin dynasty (1115-1234) and in the process plundered the Song palace of its treasures. For this reason, scholars of the Southern Song period having fewer real artefacts to consult, concentrated even more strongly on the form and content of rubbed inscriptions. This is reflected in the 1144 *Li dai zhong ding yi qi kuan zhi fa tie* ('Copies of Inscriptions on Bells, Cups and Vessels Throughout the History of China') by Xue Shanggong, which was probably the last book to be written on epigraphy during the Song. Its purist approach was later greatly esteemed during the Qing dynasty (1644-1911).

During the Yuan and Ming dynasties (1280-1367 and 1368-1644), changes in the academic climate meant that the study of ancient objects through archaeology became less popular. For this reason there are almost no new catalogues of bronzes; indeed, many of the foremost Song publications like the *Kao gu tu* and the *Bo gu tu lu* were reprinted several times during the Ming dynasty. These were the centuries when many of the best books on the philosophy of taste were produced (see below), works which give different perspectives on the shape and function of bronze vessels.

However, there is one catalogue or group of associated catalogues which should
6 be discussed here. The main work is called *Xuande yi qi tu pu* ('Illustrated Catalogue of the Ritual Vessels of the Xuande Period'), which purports to be the wording of an imperial decree of 1428 ordering bronzes for the palace, and which illustrates these vessels. It is stated there that in 1427 the emperor received from the King of Thailand a tribute of 39,000 catties of copper (about 23 tons). In the next year he commanded this metal to be used to make ritual vessels for the imperial altars and for other agreed destinations within the palace. The Board of Rites and the Board of Works were ordered to proceed with this work using the *Kao gu tu* and the *Bo gu tu lu* (see p. 14 above) as models.[11] Despite this injunction, few of the vessels imitated ancient pieces as illustrated in the two Song catalogues. Several reasons, not least the fact that this decree is nowhere mentioned in the official Ming history, are adduced to question the authenticity of the *Xuande yi qi tu pu*.[12] From inconsistencies in the dated preface of 1428 and in the dated postscript of 1534, it has been concluded that both are false and that they may not have been written much before 1600. The contents of the catalogue itself are less easy to attribute, although it seems likely that they are also of seventeenth century date. The illustrations that have come down to us do not necessarily belong to a time before about 1900, though they may be based on earlier prototypes. It has been remarked elsewhere that late Ming scholars were notorious for their fabrication of spurious early texts,[13] while it is interesting to note that during the late 1500s and early 1600s
15 various Ming authors included frequent mention of 'Xuande censers' in their

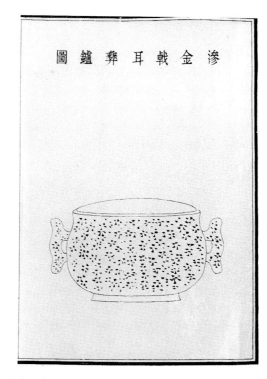

6 *Illustration from Xuande yi qi tu pu, juan 13, p. 2, showing bronze censer with gold splash decoration. Courtesy of the Percival David Foundation of Chinese Art.*

writings, indicating that these were recognised and valued types.

Whatever the truth about the dating of the Xuande bronze catalogue may be, the illustrations and descriptions it contains correspond closely to the large number of extant 'Xuande' bronzes, particularly the incense burners. The problem, of course, is to decide which if any are of fifteenth century date and which are later Ming and Qing reproductions. Up till now, there appears to have been little more than subjective criteria of quality to rely on. It would seem that Chinese researchers are faced with similar problems, for the recent publication of an example from the collection in the imperial palace in Peking was accompanied by a description assessing it as genuine. The judgement was based on consideration of form, colour and the similarity of the mark to that on Xuande porcelain.[14] The difficulties of such assessment become acute when considering examples in the V&A's collection, for example those illustrated in Plate 15. The existence of a number of later copies is demonstrated by several bronzes, including one which actually bears a Kangxi mark.

7 *Bronze censer with gold splash decoration,* 16th–17th century, height 10.1 cm, J. de Lopes Bequest, M.268-1929.

周古仲尊

Above:
8   *Illustration from Xi Qing gu jian,* compiled in 1749. This edition 1908, *juan 9,* p. 9.

Left:
9   *Wine vessel (zun),* imitation of an ancient bronze, 18th–19th century, height 20 cm, Eumorfopoulos Collection, M.184–1935.

After the founding of the Qing dynasty in 1644 textual research came to be valued anew and both the learned and the rich started to amass, study and publish their bronzes again. A host of Qing catalogues were compiled by private collectors,[15] while the Qing imperial court formed such a huge collection that several consecutive chronicles were needed. The Qing palace bronze annals are called *Xi Qing gu jian* ('Mirror of Antiquities (prepared in) the Xi Qing (Hall)') and were originally published in 1749 with three later sequels.[16] Their format is based on the Song work *Bo gu tu lu,* so that vessels all have individual names and together with mirrors and coins are depicted in line drawing with great detail. They are divided according to period (none save the coins and mirrors admitting.to a date later than the Han dynasty), and are accompanied as usual by rubbings of inscriptions, and details of size and weight. Looking at the printed pages, it is difficult to distinguish ancient pieces from later copies. This exquisitely illustrated series of books must have played a major part in supplying form and decoration to the antique fakers.

The works described so far are illustrated. We shall now consider some books which, although without pictures, contain a wealth of information on bronzes both archaic and modern. The first private encyclopaedic catalogues were published in

8, 9
10, 11
12, 13

10   *Illustration from Xi Qing gu jian,* compiled in 1749. This edition 1908, *juan* 13, p. 21.

11   *Food vessel (gui),* imitation of an ancient bronze, 18th–19th century, height 10.1 cm, 203-1899.

21

the Tang dynasty (618-906) and some of the best known appeared between the late Song and early Ming periods (thirteenth to fifteenth centuries).

Zhao Xigu was a member of the Song imperial family, known to have been writing in the years around 1230. He is the author of *Dong tian qing lu ji* (usually translated as 'Conspectus of Criticism of Antiques').[17] This early work describes several aspects of connoisseurship which were referred to again by later authors. These include the colour and appearance of different forms of patina, the style of inscriptions and the manner in which they were cast, and the casting of the vessels themselves (Zhao presumed that all archaic pieces used the lost-wax method, which would have been employed in his own time, see p. 68). He mentions one test which I have seen utilised by contemporary Chinese scholars, namely that of smell:

> Ancient vessels of the Xia, Shang and Zhou dynasties (about 2000-221 BC)
> do not have the slightest rank odour, though those that are newly excavated
> have an earthy smell that disappears in time. If a vessel is a fake and is rubbed
> in the warmed palms of the hands a terrible stink of bronze arises.[18]

Zhao believed in two magical properties of old bronzes which no doubt had their origins in the distant past and which were to be repeated many times in the future; firstly, that they warded off evil spirits because of their immense age and should thus be kept in every home, and secondly, that they were good for flower-arranging because they kept blooms fresh. Most interestingly, Zhao cites vessels of recent date and includes the earliest known detailed recipe for forgery.

Published in Nanking in 1388, the *Ge gu yao lun* ('Essential Criteria of Antiquities') by Cao Zhao, with Wang Zuo's revisions of 1459, is a well-known work.[19] Cao includes similar comments to those of Zhao on the colour, patination and casting of bronzes, on recent pieces, and on the efficacy of ancient vessels as repellants of evil spirits and for keeping flowers fresh. His recipe for faking is brief, but he does mention incense burners for the first time (see p. 33), and in another section discusses metals like gold and the forgery of precious metals. A later note on the manuscript confirms a further quality that ancient pieces were held to possess, namely a pleasant note when struck:

> . . . the tone of an ancient bronze is sonorous, that of a modern bronze
> muted.[20]

In the later Ming period of the sixteenth to seventeenth centuries, there was a proliferation of works on fashion and taste; they have been called 'handbooks of elegant living'. The style leaders who wrote them were drawn from the ranks of élite scholar-gentlemen living mainly in the Jiangnan area of southern central China. They detail what the fastidious connoisseur would surround himself with in daily life, and although their barbed pronouncements do not always concur, many passages were borrowed freely and quoted verbatim.[21] Out of several such books I shall mention four.

Zun sheng ba jian ('Eight Discourses on the Art of Living') by Gao Lian was first published in 1591, the eight discourses of the title being concerned with personal well-being. One section of the book is entitled 'Refined Enjoyment of Elegant Leisure',[22] and in it Gao specifically mentions and quotes Cao Zhao on bronzes. His

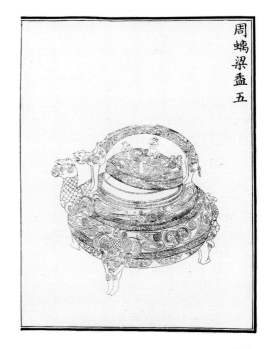

12 *Illustration from Xi Qing gu jian,* compiled in 1749. This edition 1908, *juan* 31, p. 58.

Opposite page:
13 *Pouring vessel,* bronze inlaid with gold and silver and copying an ancient vessel, Yuan-Ming dynasty, height 21 cm, 227-1879.

detailed description of forgery is prefaced by the names of places where modern fakes were made and contains interesting information on composite vessels (see p. 74). In a section called 'Discussion of Xuande and Japanese bronze incense burners and vases' Gao does just that, proving that the Xuande censer was a well-known and valued item by his day. The 'Japanese' pieces are the topic of an interesting tale about a certain bronze-worker called Pan, who as a child was captured by pirates and taken to Japan where he learned his craft. On his return home he actually worked in the Gao home for a number of years, indicating that Japanese techniques were much admired during that period. Gao remarks that such pieces fetched high prices.[23]

Variations on the bronze theme are made in works like Zhang Yingwen's *Qing bi cang* ('Treasury of Clear and Abstruse Matters') and Tu Long's essays. Tu Long (1542-1605) was an eccentric poet, dramatist and one-time civil servant, who wrote several essays on high living and the collection of art objects.[24] Zhang (1530-94) was a dilettante resident in Suzhou, at the centre of the antiquarian market. He mentions Xuande censers as desirable collector's items, and colour-codes ancient bronze patinas in order of desirability:

Best are those of dark brown colour, worst are those of lead colour.
Brown pieces with cinnabar-coloured mottled patches are better than those that are simply cinnabar-coloured. These are not as good as those of a green colour, which are not as good as those of a blue-green colour, which in turn are not as good as those that are mercury-coloured [i.e. pale silver-grey]. Mercury-coloured bronzes are not as good as those the colour of black lacquer, notwithstanding the fact that lacquer-black pieces are the easiest to fake . . .[25]

Wen Zhenheng (1585-1645), great-grandson of the distinguished Ming painter Wen Zhengming, wrote a book called *Zhang wu zhi* ('Treatise on Superfluous Things')[26] which has been descibed as the most complete work on all objects dear to the cultured scholar.[27] His material on bronzes is in the main unoriginal, but interesting because it discusses Xuande censers, as well as flower vases, the latter in terms common to other flower-arranging manuals:

In spring and winter one should use bronze, in autumn and summer porcelain. In the main hall one should use large vases, and in the library small ones. Bronze and porcelain are to be valued, gold and silver abhorred. Vases with ring handles should be avoided, as should matching pairs of vases. Slender elegant pieces are appropriate, over-elaborate pieces are not . . .[28]

Related to the 'handbooks of elegant living' but standing a little apart from them are several treatises devoted to flower-arranging. This civilised pursuit was first written about in the Song period, in relatively straightforward terms which described how to display flowers and keep them alive longer. By the Ming dynasty, writers had developed ideas relating to the arranging process and to the vessels used to display flowers in which had become just as important, if not more so, as the flowers themselves.[29] The art of flower-arranging cemented strong links between the craft traditions of China and Japan from the Tang dynasty onwards. By the late

Opposite page:
14 *Two bronze vases,* 12th-14th century, heights 23.5 cm and 20.5 cm, 5403-1901 and 91-1876. Vases with ring handles like these two were condemned as vulgar by several Ming dynasty connoisseurs.

Song period the Japanese were importing Chinese bronzes, were copying them and were evolving their own techniques.

The son of the writer Zhang Yingwen, mentioned above, was Zhang Chou. He composed *Ping hua pu* ('Monograph on the Art of Putting Flowers in Vases') whose preface is dated 1595, a 'rather dry technical monograph by a mediocre scholar'.[30] Several familiar themes emerge, such as the notion that flowers keep better in old bronzes that have been buried underground for centuries. His 'classification of vases' runs as follows:

As a general rule, and in order to display and keep flowers fresh, the choice of vase is most important. In spring and winter one should use bronze, in autumn and summer porcelain. In the main hall one should use a large vase, and in the library a small one. It is refined to put porcelain and bronze above gold and silver. One should never use vases with ring handles or in matching pairs, because they have the air of a religious cult. The mouth of the vase should be small, while the base should be thick to ensure stability, without impairing its essential elegance . . . Bronze forms that are good for flower-arranging are *zun*, *lei*, *gu* and *hu*. The vessels that men of ancient times used for wine are those that seem today most appropriate for flowers.

14

Ping shi ('Treatise on (Flower) Vases') is a livelier work, the 'mannered treatise of a rather precious individual, sketched with a musk-scented paintbrush'.[31] Written by Yuan Hongdao around 1605, it repeats many of Zhang Chou's strictures in more vehement tones:

14

What Must be Avoided When Arranging a Vase of Flowers. You must avoid vases with ring handles, matching pairs, jars with small mouths and drug pots with thin belly and foot. You should avoid as a general rule vases in gourd form, and carved stools or stools painted with flower patterns. You should not put vases on low tables without fixing them down in case they get knocked over . . . You should avoid the fumes of burning perfumed incense and coal. You should guard against depredations by cats and rats.

In the section on utensils Yuan catalogues desirable items, most of them rare and costly things like ancient bronzes. An interesting perspective to the very, very high price that archaic bronzes commanded is provided when he remarks that:

The poor scholar has no means of obtaining such luxuries. If all he can get hold of is a piece of Xuande or Chenghua porcelain [relatively modern wares in Yuan's time], then he should be regarded as an upstart beggar!

Perhaps the most famous account of flower-arranging in the Qing dynasty (1644-1911) is that of Shen Fu, who wrote his *Fu sheng liu ji* ('Six Records of a Floating Life') in 1809.[32] The 'records', which cover major events in his life, include in the second section a description of how to create a *penjing* (literally, 'landscape in a dish', a miniaturised arrangement originated by the Chinese but better known in the west by the Japanese term *bonsai*). He also stipulates conditions for flower arrangements:

From three to seven vases can be arranged on a table, depending on its size. No more than seven vases should be set out on one table, or it will not be

15 *Two bronze censers with gold splash decoration,* mark of the Xuande period (1426-35) but dating to the 16th-17th century, heights 5.5 cm and 11.5 cm, J. de Lopes Bequest, M.270 & 269-1929.

possible to tell the eyes from the eyebrows, and the arrangement will look
just like the cheap chrysanthemum screens sold in the markets . . .

The Qing period saw a vast increase in many branches of literature, among them
the *bi ji* or short, connected essays so beloved by connoisseurs and collectors. A
mature example of the type is *Chi bei ou tan* ('Chance Gossip from North of the
Pool') by government official and poet Wang Shizhen, which was published in
1701.[33] Wang devotes a whole section to Xuande period censers and water
droppers, including accounts of such rumoured events as the fire in a Buddha hall in
the palace during the Xuande period (1426-35) which melted down gold, silver and
bronze figures, the resultant intermingled metal being used to cast vessels.
Unfortunately, this tale can neither be metallurgically nor historically
corroborated.[34] Wang distinguishes between real and fake pieces on the basis of
colour; genuine examples having a good colour right the way through, but fake
ones shamming a patina on the outside only. He mentions two Ming 'schools' of
bronze-casting, a northern and a southern one, and has some interesting things to
say about forgeries.

Wang Yingkui's *Liunan sui bi* ('Master Liunan's Jottings') was published in
1740.[35] It repeats the legend of the palace fire, and several other anecdotes used by
Wang Shizhen. Of Xuande censers he remarks:

In colour you can distinguish between early, middle and late; early pieces
imitate Song mottled tones, middle-period pieces use imported minerals and
come out tea-coloured with gold patches, while late ones are plainer and
more dull and pale in tone.

Xie Kunpan was active in the Daoguang period (1821-50), and in his *Quan yu suo sui*
('Complete Compendium of Jades') chose to discuss the humble bronze wash-
basin:

There are red ones and azure ones and brown ones, and there are pieces
mottled with cinnabar-red colour. Some have twin fish designs, some twin
dragons, and some have one fish and one dragon. There are basins with date
marks that show the year and lunar month, and others with good luck
mottoes like 'great good fortune' and 'riches, honour, and many sons and
grandsons' . . . I bought a brown-coloured one in Taiyuan that weighed
eight catties, twelve ounces, with no inscription but a design of twin
fishes.[36]

It is interesting that such simple vessels, which have been excavated in some
numbers from Song, Yuan and Ming dynasty tombs should be accounted
collectors' items by the early nineteenth century.

It is not proposed to discuss here analytical works of the late Qing and
Republican periods since they have no direct relevance to the bronzes in this book.
From the 1940s a large body of new material has become available to us in the form
of archaeological reports. Their findings will be used as evidence in the following
chapters.

16 *Two bronze incense stick holders,*
    12th–14th century, heights 15 cm, and
    9.5 cm, 170 & 138-1876.

Vessel Forms

Censers, *jue* and vases

Among the vessels illustrated in this book two main groupings may be distinguished. The first group consists of pieces that were used on temple or domestic altars and in tombs; excavation and pictorial evidence show that similar arrangements were used in all three. These ceremonial vessels may be said to be linked in their hieratic usage with archaic bronzes from the distant past, although their forms are not entirely similar. The second group comprises pieces that were used in everyday life, either for domestic or decorative purposes. This division is necessarily a broad one for it includes not only humble items like wash-basins, but also the choice collectors' objects favoured by Wen Zhenheng and others of the scholar-élite. There was also a crossover in usage among items like flower vases which were used both on altars and in the libraries of those aesthetes who were often expert flower-arrangers.

The usual arrangement of vessels on an altar comprised five vessels *(wu gong)*, a central censer flanked by pairs of candlesticks and vases. Relatively few candlesticks survive. Both censers and vases, because of their multiplicity of usages, are more common. The grandest sets of vessels were those made for palace use and for the halls of wealthy laymen and monks. The scale of such castings is illustrated by a set of regulations governing the building and furnishing of imperial palaces between 1727 and 1750 which survives in manuscript form.[37] Under a section entitled 'Rules for making sacrificial vessels and ornaments for temple use', we learn that the largest temple in the Yuan Ming Yuan (the imperial summer palace in Peking) was furnished with the following: a 'size 1' censer measuring 40 cm by 30 cm and 28 cm high with censer stand; a pair of candlesticks 60 cm high with stands; a pair of incense sticks and holders, and a pair of lotus vases 58 cm high with stands. Subsidiary halls had similar vessel sets ranging down from 'size 2' to 'size 4'.[38]

It would have been easier to carry out casting on this scale on site, and elsewhere in the same text we learn of the amounts of coal, crucibles, earth and rope that were used in proportion to every 100 catties of bronze at the foundry in the Yong He Gong (the Lama Temple) in Peking.[39] In chapter 36 under the rules for brass-making is a recipe for giving 'Xuande bronzes' an appearance of age, a practice which was evidently as important to foundrymen of the Qing age as to artisans of earlier times.[40]

Sets of altar vessels were not only to be found in the grandest places for many homes had their own halls of (usually Buddhist) worship. Even an upright Confucian scholar like Wen Zhenheng mentions the arrangement of his *fo shi* or 'Buddha chamber'.[41]

A further altar vessel, often dedicated to temples, was a container called *jue*.[42] *Jue*

16

were used during the bronze age (about 1700–1000 BC) for heating alcohol over fire, and in later times they retained their archaic form of a rounded container on three legs. Post-like handles on the rim were originally used to lift the vessel full of warmed liquid away from the heat. Illustrated are four *jue* in the V&A's collection, two dating to the early Ming period, one to the later Ming, and one to the Qing.

The three Ming dynasty pieces are shown in Plates 17 and 18. Two of them bear inscriptions, which show that both were made in the province of Guangdong. The vessel to the right of Plate 17 has four panels of inscription (on both sides, the back, and beneath the lip), which between them say:

Confucian temple.
Set up on an auspicious day in the seventh autumn month of the first year of Chenghua (1465).

17   *Three bronze altar vessels (jue),* the vessel on the left 14th–15th century, the vessel in the centre dated to 1541, the vessel on the right dated to 1465. Heights 14.5 cm, 19.9 cm, 19.5 cm. 4–1876, Day Gift FE.4–1984, FE.43-1983.

31

18   Liu Wei, commissioned with the rank of *jinshi*, Administration
      Commissioner of Guangdong and Administrative Assistant of the Right.
      Wu Zhong of Leping, commissioned with the rank of *jinshi*, Magistrate of
      Dongguan County. [43]
The vessel in the centre of Plate 17 has a single square panel of inscription that says:
18   Made on an auspicious day in the tenth month of the twentieth year of Jiajing
      (1541) at Guangzhou fu (i.e. Canton).
19 The vessel in Plate 19 has a six-character Qianlong reign period mark (1736-95) in
    sealscript on the base.

    It is perhaps significant that the two earlier vessels are made from copper/tin
alloys (bronze) while the two later ones are made from copper/zinc alloys (brass)
(see p. 36). All of them have carelessly worked decoration and are made of fairly
low-grade metal; at least one seems to be partially composed of scrap metal. It
would appear that votive vessels for small temples must have been relatively cheap
to buy.

    As has been mentioned above, censer and vase forms were also put to secular use.
Speaking first of censers, we should note that incense was first used in China as a
form of fumigation. It was employed to disperse insect pests, while at the same time
being totally harmless and giving out a pleasant odour. As early as the Zhou period
(1027-221 BC) artemisia was burned, its dense clouds of fragrant smoke also serving
to mask unpleasant smells. Several Ming dynasty authors comment on the fact that

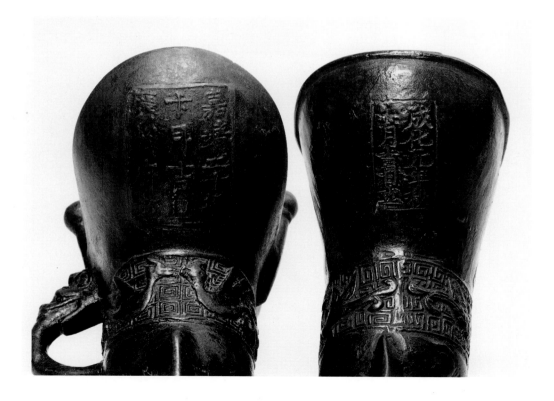

18 *Inscriptions on two of the altar vessels in*
    Plate 17.

32

19 *Bronze altar vessel (jue),* reign mark of Qianlong (1736–95), height 17.8 cm, M.6-1929.

archaic bronzes did not include specific vessels in which to burn incense and that ancient *yi, ding* and *gui* which were used for that purpose in later times were not performing their original function.[44]

During the Qin and Han dynasties (221 BC–AD 220) many philosophers sought to achieve the secret of immortality; there were reputed to exist several homes of the Immortals, islands of paradise on earth. Expeditions were actually launched to go in search of them, some of the doughty voyagers ending up in Japan. Incense burners in the shape of island paradises were made, which when used would throw up clouds of vapour from their slopes. These censers were usually ceramic but also occurred in bronze, sometimes inlaid with gold or precious stones. Both vegetable and animal incenses were burnt in them, the plant incenses including cassia,

33

camphor, liquorice and fennel, while the animal kingdom supplied such perfumes as civet and musk. From the Tang period (618-906) onwards imported fragrances such as sandalwood, garuwood, ambergris and gum benzoin supplemented the indigenous incense perfumes. The incense came in the form of small sticks or cones, which were embedded in a layer of sand or ash in the censer base.

20   By the Song period (960-1279) a wide range of censers were available. The example in Plate 20 has three-dimensional decoration of dragons with a flaming pearl. It is an example of the general use of dragons as decorative motifs, when they were clearly not symbols of imperial ownership. Relief patterns like these are also found on Song dynasty ceramic burial jars, while the monster-mask legs and spiral pattern beneath the rim match that on excavated bronze artefacts (although this pattern continued in later times as well).[45]

21   The form of the censer in Plate 21, with its tall handles, was a popular one. Large incense burners in this shape are found in temple and palace complexes. It is a difficult piece to attribute; comparison with a range of different examples and knowledge of its composition, which is mainly copper and zinc with significant amounts of lead and tin, suggest a date in the Ming dynasty.

Left:
20 *Bronze censer decorated with dragons chasing a flaming pearl,* 12th-14th century, height 9 cm, 5380-1901.

Right:
21 *Bronze censer,* Ming dynasty (1368-1644), height 11.5 cm, 5377-1901.

22   Another Ming censer, with the reign mark of the Emperor Xuande (reigned 1426–35) on the base (see below), is shown in Plate 22. It bears an auspicious pattern of small boys playing, and has a squared spiral inlaid in silver wire round the top.[46] Both the content of the design and the manner in which it is executed are comparable to Ming lacquer and carved wood.[47]

23   The plain vessel in Plate 23 stands as an archetype for all censers, and as such could date to several periods. However, the 1777 inventory for the Chinese pavilion at Drottningholm Palace, the residence of the Swedish Royal Family near Stockholm, includes a censer similar to this one.[48]

A problematic group of censers comprises those bearing the mark of the Emperor Xuande (reigned 1426–35). As has been mentioned before (p. 18), metalwork made during this reign was seen as being of exceptional quality and therefore the appearance of a Xuande mark on a piece is likely to have added to its value. An identifiable feature of most of the 'Xuande' censers in the V&A's collection is that

Left:
22   *Bronze censer with silver wire inlay round mouth and handles,* reign mark of Xuande (1426–35) but dating to the 16th–17th century, height 16.5 cm, 178-1899.

Right:
23   *Bronze censer,* 17th–18th century, height 22.5 cm, Owen Bequest, M.41-1921.

24 *Brass censer with brass stand,* reign mark of
    Xuande (1426–35) but dating to the
    16th–18th century, height with stand
    13 cm, 2729–1856.

24 they are made of brass, i.e. of an alloy of copper and zinc. Moreover, most of the
    censers, are made of an Alpha-phase brass, i.e. an alloy with a very high zinc
    content of between 29 and 35%. The profile of elements identified suggests that a
    controlled composition was being aimed at and that these alloys were made
    deliberately. Such brass censers would have been bright yellow and shiny when
    freshly polished but seem to have been allowed to acquire a natural brownish
    patina, with no evidence of having been cleaned.

    When was brass first produced in China? Some authorities have traced references
    to zinc-containing alloys back to the second century BC, and to the use of the metal
    by the ninth and tenth centuries AD.[49] However, we must distinguish here between
    brass produced by heating together metal ores in their raw state and brass produced
    by using zinc which had already been distilled. The former method is known as the
    cementation method while the latter is known as the method using metallic zinc.

    The distillation of zinc is complicated, and there is no clear textual evidence for
    the isolation of metallic zinc by the Chinese until the early seventeenth century
    AD.[50] A recent study of 550 Chinese coins showed that cash was usually

manufactured from leaded bronze until the sixteenth century.[51] Then, in the period 1503–5, brass coinage was introduced and from 1527 onwards all subsequent coins were made of brass. However, this was brass made by the cementation method (which is identified as being up to 28% zinc by weight of the total composition) rather than brass containing metallic zinc (28% and over). The latter was not introduced until the early seventeenth century.[52]

Coin manufacture often represents a rather conservative technology. Nevertheless, analytical research to date indicates that brasses made by the cementation process do not occur before the Ming dynasty; this hypothesis is strengthened by the tested composition of a range of datable Song and Yuan period vases discussed below, none of which is made of brass. Brasses containing metallic zinc probably do not occur before the sixteenth to seventeenth centuries. Thus many censers bearing Xuande marks may first have been made in the late Ming period, a time which textual evidence shows to have been busy with the manufacture of 'antiques'. The one censer in the Museum's collection with a
25 Kangxi reign mark (1662–1722) is actually made of brass, being a copper/zinc alloy with some lead and a tiny amount of tin. Analytical results suggest that metallic zinc was used.

25 *Brass censer,* reign mark of Kangxi (1662–1722), height 10.5 cm, Brooks Bequest, M.1171–1926.

26   Some of the censers have 'gold splash' decoration.[53] Examination shows this to have been achieved by fire-gilding, in other words by applying gold in the form of a gold/mercury amalgam and then heating the vessel to drive off the mercury. A small amount of gold was left adhering to the base metal since this method is particularly suitable for the application of very thin layers. The process could be repeated several times to build up layers of gold, if desired. Fire gilding is dangerous and is now banned in most countries because the mercury vapour given off is highly toxic to the gilder and is liable to escape as a poisonous vapour into the atmosphere.

We shall turn now to a discussion of vases. In the period covered by this book bronze vases were made to hold flowers, feathers and other decorative arrangements on temple altars. They were also used as containers for flower-arranging in the home.

It cannot be stressed too strongly how great was the influence of bronzes on ceramics in the Song and post-Song periods, and this influence can be observed in the form and decoration of many vessels.[54] A sequence of bronze vases displaying close stylistic parallels with Song, Yuan, Ming and Qing dynasty (960-1911) porcelains are shown here.

27   The two ceramic vases in Plate 27 are examples of *yingqing* porcelain ('shadow blue' porcelain, so-called because of the colour of the glaze) from the Jingdezhen kilns in Jiangxi province. Pairs of vases like this were often made for tomb altars because ceramic was a cheap alternative to bronze. These examples must have been quite inexpensive items for they are roughly made. They still show signs of burial dirt and by comparison with excavated examples from Chinese tombs can be dated to the Yuan dynasty (1280-1368).[55] The bronze vase in the middle of Plate 27 may also be Yuan dynasty in date. However, comparison with the vase illustrated in Plates 31, 32, 46 and 47 shows that it could date to as early as the Song dynasty, indicating that bronze forms often predated ceramic forms.

28   The two elegant bronze vases in Plate 28 are in shapes that occur amongst porcelains from the Longquan kilns in Zhejiang province. Two Longquan porcelain vases in just these shapes were dug up from a Yuan dynasty tomb in Sichuan province, a site that also yielded bronzes.[56] The pieces illustrated in Plate 28 may also date to the Yuan dynasty, or they may predate the ceramic examples and thus date to the Song dynasty.

Vases with narrow necks, 'garlic-head' tops and applied models of dragons are common in porcelain from the Dehua kilns in Fujian province. Dehua examples of similar form have been attributed to the period 1640-80.[57] The two bronze vases
29   illustrated in Plate 29 should therefore date to the sixteenth or seventeenth century.
30   The form of the bronze vase in Plate 30 is echoed in ceramics of the Qing dynasty (1644-1911).[58] When analysed, the piece indicated that it might have been made in the later Ming or Qing periods by its composition, which was an alloy of copper and zinc with tiny amounts of lead and tin, i.e. a brass. The zinc composition was high at 29%. The base plate had an entirely different composition, and had been fitted in separately. The bases of bronze vases were commonly made of inserted sheet metal at all periods from the Song dynasty (960-1279) onwards.

Opposite page:
26   *Bronze censer in form of fruit, with gold splash decoration,* wood stand and lid with jade knop. 16th-17th century, height with lid and stand 12 cm, Salting Bequest, M.734-1910.

Opposite page:
27 *Pair of porcelain altar vases from a tomb,
with bronze vase.* The porcelain vases
13th-14th century, the bronze vase
12th-14th century. Heights 23.5 cm and
28.5 cm, C.68 & 69-1910, 104-1876.

Left:
28 *Two bronze vases,* 12th-14th century,
heights 17 cm and 21 cm, 120 &
121-1876.

41

29 *Two bronze vases with dragons,* one parcel-gilt, 16th-17th century, heights 19 cm and 20 cm, M.167-1967, 88-1876.

30 *Brass vase,* 17th-18th century, height 15 cm, 147-1876.

31, 32   The vase in Plates 31, 32, 46 and 47 has been dated by inscription to 1173, the
46, 47   Song dynasty, and was the subject of an article tracing its geographical, historical, economic and decorative origins.[59] Metallurgically the piece was shown to be a copper/tin alloy with a significant percentage of lead (i.e. leaded bronze); in broad terms, this composition was standard for all Song, Jin and Yuan dynasty (960–1368)

Opposite page:

31   *Bronze vase* with inscription dated to 1173. Height 30.8 cm, Anderson Bequest, M.164-1917.

42

vases analysed by Maria Fabrizi at the V&A, although there were of course percentage variations for every vessel.

In decorative terms, the pattern bands were shown to relate to contemporary design in other media, particularly architecture and ceramics, while deriving some influence from archaic bronze. The bands were probably applied separately to a core model before casting and could thus be copied from a standard design repertory. In fact, many of the patterns on this vase are duplicated on other bronzes. Certain designs seem to have been popular for some years. For example, the curious register of repeated elements round the shoulder of this vase, which look a little like butterflies placed side by side and head to tail, but which are more probably stylised monster-masks (*taotie*), has been found on vessels excavated from Yuan dynasty (1280–1368) tombs.[60] The vase in Plate 33 has the same design above the foot.

32

33

32 *Detail of vase in Plate 31* showing pattern bands. Compare the upper pattern band with the decoration on the vase in Plate 33.

Opposite page:
33 *Bronze vase,* 12th–14th century, height 30 cm, 166–1876.

34   The two pieces in Plate 34 both bear sinuous, spiral-filled patterns which derive from interlocking dragon designs on bronzes of Eastern Zhou date (770–221 BC). Excavation in China of bronzes bearing similar patterns indicates that the two pieces date to the Song (960–1279) or Jin (1127–1234) dynasty.[61] Archaeological work in China has been the key to identification of a whole series of Song, Yuan and 35, 36 Ming bronzes. The vases in Plates 35, 36 and 37 can all be dated by reference to 37 excavated bronzes.[62]

From at least as early as the Song dynasty bronzes were exported to Korea and Japan. Korean ceramics of the Koryŏ period (918–1392) include examples influenced in both form and decoration by bronzes. The recent excavation of a ship wrecked off the southeast coast of Korea established that it was bound for Japan, carrying a cargo that included both bronzes and ceramics.[63] The ship left the Chinese port of Ningbo in the summer of 1323 and sank less than a month later.

Bronzes like those in this ship's cargo were probably initially used in Japanese temples. However, a later function was as flower vases in the various forms of tea ceremony that developed in Japan from the fourteenth century. They were also used as containers for flowers in the several schools of flower arrangement that arose in Japan, and in both these cases inspired local imitations in metal and ceramic. The tea ceremony and the arrangement of flowers were themselves stimulated by Chinese practices. Some of the seminal works on this subject were mentioned in Chapter 1. Yuan Hongdao's book of 1605, *Ping shi* ('Treatise on (Flower) Vases', see p. 26), was probably transported to Japan in the eighteenth century where it resulted in the initiation of a sect of flower-arrangers called *Kodōryū* which still exists today. It is clear that collections of tea ceremony implements and collections connected with flower-arranging in Japan must contain much material of value to the study of later Chinese bronzes. Some examples have been published,[64] but much awaits discovery.

Some of the later Chinese bronzes that were used in Japan subsequently reached Europe in rather a curious manner. In 1876, the South Kensington Museum (now 38 the Victoria and Albert Museum) purchased a large number of bronzes (about 150 pieces) from the shop of Samuel Bing in Paris. Samuel Bing later became famous for his *Salon de l'Art Nouveau*, which both gave its name to and greatly influenced the development of the international art style that we know as 'art nouveau'. Bing was born in Hamburg, but travelled to Paris before 1871, and later became a naturalised French citizen. In 1875 he went to Japan, and subsequently opened two shops in Paris as a dealer and importer of Japanese art.[65] The South Kensington Museum must have been one of his first major customers. The bronzes the Museum purchased in 1876 were all believed to be Japanese at the time. In fact, many are Chinese, some of them archaic pieces but many more dating to the Song and Yuan dynasties. This is further proof of the huge quantity of Chinese bronzes that must have entered Japan in earlier times. From Japan they were exported to France by Samuel Bing and by this roundabout route finally reached London.

The vases discussed so far have all been made of bronze and were made for altars 39 or for domestic use as flower containers. Included here is a rather different sort of vase made of iron. The form of this vessel is known in Chinese as *tou hu* 'pitch pot', and it developed in very early times for use in a popular game. The game involved throwing arrows into a pot, different marks being awarded depending on whether the arrows landed in the wider mouth opening or in the lugs on the side. The 'pitch pot' game was recorded as early as the sixth century BC.[66] By the time this vase was made in the late Ming dynasty[67] such pieces were possibly made for display in temples or palaces and not for playing games with. Many Yuan and Ming dynasty (1280-1644) ceramic examples of the form are known.

The piece in Plate 39 is made of cast iron and is decorated with a relief pattern of flowers and leaves. The raised ridges where the piece was jointed together, and the raised criss-cross pattern round the base section, were probably used to anchor the gesso and coloured pigment which originally decorated the surface. Cast iron vessels and statues have a rough, unfinished look which is puzzling unless one

39 *Cast iron vase (tou hu or 'pitch pot'),* 16th century, height 50.5 cm, M.553-1911.

understands that their raised seams were coated with a gesso ground and painted over. Some iron pieces retain traces of their surface decoration, but many have been scoured clean. The loss of surface sometimes occurs through time and wear, but one suspects that some examples were scoured clean before being sold, to get rid of flaking, uneven surfaces. This vase no longer bears any traces of its original surface.

Left:
37 *Bronze vase,* 12th–14th century, height 14 cm, 5392-1901.

Right:
38 *Bronze vase,* 12th–14th century, height 26 cm, 186-1876. This is one of many bronzes acquired by the Museum from the shop of Samuel Bing in Paris in 1876.

Pieces with Inlaid Decoration

One of the most interesting categories of later bronze is that inlaid with gold and silver. Inlaid pieces are often difficult to date. It has been suggested that some quite magnificent inlaid pieces in the V&A date to the Song dynasty (960-1279), the judgement being made on the basis of form and style.[68] Recent thermoluminescence analysis of a small group of inlaid vessels at Oxford indicated a range of dates from late Song to the present century.[69] The attribution of inlaid pieces seems to be a complex problem, which visual examination alone will not resolve. It is difficult to distinguish, for example, between pieces which when tested gave a Song dynasty date, and those which gave a seventeenth century date.

One vessel which tests showed to be of relatively early date was an inlaid goose censer, very similar to that illustrated in Plates 4 and 5.[70] The plain metal of the vessel in Plates 4 and 5 proved to be an alloy of copper and tin, with some lead. The elaborate inlays consisted of both silver and gold sheet metal, and wires. All three types of inlay were inserted into pre-chiselled depressions in the surface of the bronze. The areas prepared to receive the larger sheet inlays seem to have been slightly undercut round the edges, in order to hold the inlays more securely. The wire-work seems to have been carried out separately from the sheet-work, as some junctions between the two show slight gaps.

All the pieces in the Museum's collection with this style of inlay also appear to have been given considerable surface treatment to enhance their patinas; heaped-up areas of added cinnabar and malachite are common. The vessels in Plate 40 show many of the features just discussed. The censer in the middle of Plate 40 (M.726-1910), when thermoluminescence tested at Oxford, gave a provisional dating of between about 1600 and 1720.[71]

A late Ming to early Qing date is possibly significant when we consider how some inlaid bronzes were used. All the vessels illustrated in Plate 40 are small, and during the Qing dynasty (1644-1911) collectors are said to have devoted much time to amassing miniature treasures which they kept in curio cabinets. These curio containers, which could be cabinets but also cases, chests or boxes, were fitted out with a series of small compartments. Each compartment was specially constructed to fit the treasures it contained. These treasures included tiny paintings, porcelains, carvings in a variety of materials and small bronzes. Many of the bronzes that survive in curio collections were inlaid with gold and silver and heavily patinated in different colours.[72] It seems that inlaid bronzes were treasured by collectors of miniature curios.

Another style of inlay is seen on the pieces in Plates 41 and 54, which have simpler designs carried out mainly in silver wire. Although the patterns on the censer in

4, 5
40
41, 54

Opposite page:
40 *Three bronzes with gold and silver inlays.* The vessels copy archaic bronzes and have artificial patination. Heights 7 cm, 16 cm, 14 cm, Brooks Bequest M.1193-1926, Salting Bequest M.726-1910, Circ.576-1927.

Plate 41 are based on ancient bronze designs they are interpreted in a bold, schematic fashion. The use of a squared spiral band in silver wire over the handles recalls that seen on the late Ming censer in Plate 22.[73] The hornless dragons that writhe in an interlocking pattern across the surface of the vase in Plate 54 have parallels among other late Ming crafts.[74] This vase also has surface accretions caused by the maker's efforts to artificially age and patinate his product.

Inlaid bronzes have interested many scholars. Most early writers took the mistaken view that vessels of the mythical Xia dynasty (about 2000–1700 BC) and of the Shang dynasty (about 1700–1027 BC), were inlaid. Zhao Xigu (thirteenth century) actually points out that in his time inlaid bronze was mistakenly held to be of Shang date. Cao Zhao (1388) agrees that Shang vessels were plain and unadorned but that Xia pieces were often inlaid with gold wire as thin as hair. Gao Lian (1591) puts them both right:

> The Xia used fine silver wire to inlay cloud and thunder patterns, even finer than the patterns on incised jade *bi*. Cao (Zhao) said that the Shang had no inlay techniques, but in fact they did, using a lot of sheet gold and silver inlay and a lesser amount of wire inlay. However, these fine inlay skills can be faked by contemporary artisans. The gold and silver used during the Xia and Shang periods is the same colour as that used today and thus can be imitated.[75]

This passage indicates that inlaid pieces were already admired in the Song period, and that they were certainly being copied by the Ming. Gao Lian goes on to praise the skills of modern Suzhou inlay work; pieces like those illustrated in Plates 40 and 41 may have been what he had in mind.

The most famous examples of intricate gilded and inlaid work are those bearing the mark Hu Wenming and associated family marks.[76] The works are usually signed as being by 'Hu Wenming of Yunjian', Yunjian being present-day Songjiang in Jiangsu province. Bronzes from the Hu workshops are valued today, and reference is often made to an anonymous Ming book of unknown date *Yunjian zazhi* ('Yunjian Records')[77] which comments admiringly on the skill, elegance and desirability of Hu's work and on the high prices that they fetched. Other commentators are not so complimentary. Dedicated aesthete Wen Zhenheng, writing in about 1620, remarks:

> Above all one should avoid vulgar bronzes made by Pan [Tie] and Hu [Wenming] of Yunjian like those with eight lucky symbols, or Japanese landscapes, or hundred nail-heads.[78]

One can perhaps understand Wen's strictures when looking at pieces like the small gilded box in Plate 42, which although finely worked presents rather a glittering appearance with its parcel-gilding.

The inlaid censer in Plate 43 is also of Ming date and although it has a Xuande mark (1426–35) its Arabic inscription suggests that it may date to the sixteenth century, as do some porcelain objects with Islamic inscriptions and Xuande marks. The religious inscription seems to have been reproduced by a craftsman unfamiliar with Arabic and was probably copied by a Chinese. It says 'day of resurrection' in

41 *Bronze censer with gold and silver inlays,
    16th–17th century, height 10.4 cm,
    FE.43-1980.*

Arabic. The composition of the censer is a copper/zinc alloy (i.e. a brass) with lead
and impurities of tin, antimony, silver, arsenic, iron, and nickel, which are typical
of impurities in copper but which may indicate recycled metal. The accompanying
jug is made of slightly different bronze, having a high zinc content and few
impurities. The inscription, again copied by a non-Arab hand, says 'resurrection,
Truth', 'Truth' being one of the ninety-nine names of Allah. Curiously, this
Islamic inscription is accompanied by a Taoist *yin-yang* symbol in the band below

42 *Bronze box and cover, parcel-gilt,* signed Zhu Chenming, 16th–17th century, diameter 9 cm, 2727-1856.

Below:
43 *Bronze censer and jug with gold and silver inlays,* with reign mark of Xuande (1426–35) but dating to the 16th–17th century. Width 8.7 cm and height 9.2 cm, FE.110, FE.109-1975.

54

the rim. The rather thin quality of gold and silver inlay on both these pieces is different in appearance to other, more opulent inlays (Plates 4 and 40).

During the Ming period bronze was not the only metal to be used for inlay work. Illustrated in Plates 44 and 45 are two vessels made of iron and inlaid with silver wire. The unusual globular jar in Plate 44 is one of a number of such pieces known. The body is riveted with four stout plates running from neck to foot, with between them panels containing further rivetted ornaments. The nature of the rivetted appliqués suggests an armourer's work. The whole surface is enriched with silver inlay, whose dominant motifs are roundels containing simplified forms of the character *shou*, meaning 'long life'. On the base of the vase is an inlaid mark of the Wanli reign period (1573-1620). The vase in Plate 45 is a simpler and more elegant creation. Both its shape, and the character of its dragon–with–bifurcated–tail and diaper pattern, suggest a Ming dynasty date.[79]

Metals and Metal-workers

Later Chinese bronzes were compounded of the metals copper and tin with variable inclusions of iron, lead and zinc. Other trace elements like antimony may be present in small quantities. The precious metals gold and silver were used for gilding and inlay work, and mercury was used in the process of gilding. It is interesting to consider where the main deposits of metal ores in China are located and which areas were documented as being active in different periods.

China produces a lot of tin, and in fact by the 1970s was contributing 4.6% of the world's supply.[80] The richest deposits are in the south, and by the eleventh century annual outputs of about 1,400 tons were already being recorded.[81] Lead and zinc are chiefly extracted today from the southern provinces of Hunan, Anhui, Jiangxi and Yunnan. The major deposits of lead are in southern Yunnan, although Guangdong province made substantial contributions in past times. Mercury comes from Guizhou and Hunan, while China produces nearly 20% of the world's supply of antimony from central Hunan, Guangxi and Guangdong. Iron, important for the making of weapons and agricultural tools as well as statues and utensils, was mined in many areas of China, the most important being the provinces of Shanxi, Shandong, Hebei, and Guangdong.

Copper lodes in China are widely scattered but small and production remained deficient into modern times.[82] The mineral deposits themselves were generally excellent but their mining was often badly managed. The main production centres in the twentieth century lie in the central province of Hubei, in the far western provinces of Yunnan and Gansu, and in north-eastern Liaoning. Liaoning was already active by the tenth century, for in 928 the Liao Emperor Taizu is recorded as having removed four thousand families from Bohai to Liaoyang, where a quarter of them were forced to open mines and pay mining taxes.

The succeeding Northern Song period (960–1127) was a fruitful time for mining expansion. The industry was encouraged by the removal of state monopoly over certain deposits, which increased revenue considerably. In 1064 and 1067 officials were sent out to inspect mines, and reported a total of 271 mines and smelting-works treating gold, silver, copper, iron, lead and tin. A remarkable amount of copper was extracted in the Song period given that Yunnan, the chief copper-producing area in later years, had not yet been conquered. It was not until 1253 that China's Mongol rulers conquered the kingdom of Dali and brought Yunnan under the sovereignty of China.

By 1102 important advances in metallurgy ensured improvements in output.[83] By 1126, on the eve of invasion by Nuzhen Tartars from the north, Song political and economic power was at its weakest and copper revenue had sunk back down to a low level. A similar pattern of peaks and troughs in production was to follow in subsequent periods.

Iron was mined in many areas during the Song period, the most important of which were Shanxi and Guangdong. By 1111 the art of smelting iron with coal is recorded in Shanxi, where deposits were so rich that more than 800 families were forcibly moved there to develop mining in 1236 and 1237. Guangdong reported ninety-two iron mines and smelters in one district in 1116 where the enormous output completely exhausted deposits, forcing the mines to close in the following year. Because of its importance in making weapons and agricultural tools iron production was the frequent target of official sanction.

The Song dynasty also saw an increase in gold and silver revenues, although deposits remained localised and small.

After the Song had been driven south by the invading Jin dynasty rulers in 1127 mineral development in the north fell behind. Mines south of the Yangtse were
31, 32 encouraged but overall output of all metal ores diminished. The vase in Plates 31,
46, 47 32, 46 and 47 was inscribed in 1173 at the southern town of Zhenjiang, and both its inscription and its components analysis tell us something about the production of bronze vessels during the Southern Song dynasty (1127-1279).[84] The inscription, which was engraved onto the pre-cast body in a sequence of dots, reads:

47   Number twenty. Registered after application with the official in charge of
    tax affairs, Zhenjiang fu, tenth day of the third month [a lunar reckoning] of
    the fourth year of the Qiandao reign [i.e. 1173].

The inscription finishes with a *hua ya,* or official signature. Analysis of the vase revealed it to be made of an alloy comprising 75.8% copper, 11.6% tin, 0.28% iron, 10.7% lead, 0.09% manganese and 1.5% arsenic.

This vase was made in the mid-twelfth century, a time when mineral resources in China were low. The decline in the supply of copper and tin coincided with a vastly increased demand for metal to mint coins. The situation was aggravated by galloping inflation and by the efflux of copper coins across both northern and southern borders to the 'barbarians' beyond, who were eager for Chinese copper coinage.[85] Various preventive methods had been tried, including the debasement of coinage, the introduction of iron and paper money, and restrictive orders on the export of copper cash.[86] When these methods failed to work, the government exercised its power to prohibit the casting of copper for household use and later extended the prohibition to cover bronze artefacts already in use. Hundreds of tons of bronze were melted down at the mints, and to inspire his subjects, in 1154 the Emperor himself sent 1,500 bronze objects from the Palace collection to the imperial mint. Certain items escaped confiscation, among them vessels for temple use. Such pieces had to be registered, as was the vase in Plates 31, 32, 46 and 47, and they were liable for taxation. However, by the mid-thirteenth century the market had recovered, the legal price of copper exceeded the value of cast goods once more, and copper coins are recorded as being transmuted into vessels.[87]

The melting down of vessels into coins and the conversion of coinage into vessels took place during most periods of Chinese history. In the sixteenth century novel

46 *Bronze vase* with inscription dated to 1173. Height 30.8 cm, Anderson Bequest, M.164–1917.

49 *Bronze seal vermilion box and three seals,
    inlaid with silver wire.* Mark *Shi sou,*
    16th–17th century. Diameter of box
    6 cm, length of seals 4.5 cm. Given by
    the Royal Asiatic Society,
    M.605F,G,H,I-1924.

The Qing artisan Qian Datian worked at Jiading, to the east of Suzhou, making bronze vessels that were reckoned to be indistinguishable from ancient pieces. His son Qian Bingtian continued the tradition. Du Shibo undertook the minor work of making stamped bronze buttons at Jiading.

Another city known for its metal products was Nanking. Gan Wentang, who cast bronze censers there during the Wanli period (1573–1620) was said to be a 'southern caster'. Feng Xiyu made inlaid bronzes during the Qing period.

Suzhou and Nanking are both in Jiangsu province. Jiangsu was one of the provinces that together formed a region known as Jiangnan, the area 'south of the river'. Jiangnan also encompassed Anhui, Jiangxi and Zhejiang provinces. Two well-known names are associated with the region; Shi Sou and Hu Wenming. Less well known are Zhang Aochun who made iron *ruyi* inlaid with silver wire, and Tang Ziyang and Hu Si who cast bronze censers during the late Ming to early Qing years.

49, 50   The case of Shi Sou bronzes is an interesting one and serves as an example of how bronze-making businesses may have operated. Illustrated in Plates 49 and 50 are two groups of small bronze implements inlaid with silver wire. Most pieces bearing the name Shi Sou ('Old man Shi') are bronzes inlaid with siver wire. All of the objects shown here were made for the desk and resemble other assemblages dating to the late Ming period.[97]

Although the items came into the Museum at different times, and can be seen to bear different designs, all have the inlaid mark *Shi sou*. In addition, items from all the groups are remarkably homogeneous in their metal composition which is copper alloyed with both tin and zinc and also containing lead, similar to gunmetal. The quantity of lead present indicates that all were made by casting and that the lead must have been a deliberate addition. The water-pot in Plate 50 was actually made in two pieces with a join round the middle and shows signs of turning after it was cast, perhaps as a method of finishing and of hiding the join. The artefacts illustrated are only part of the total number of Shi Sou artefacts acquired by the V&A, and in turn represent only a fraction of examples with a Shi Sou signature known.

Does that mean that Shi Sou was an incredibly prolific individual artisan or that he headed a very large workshop? Research into European medieval craft production practices, for which unlike Chinese there is primary source material, suggests a third possibility.[98] Many crafts were demand-led, so that both supply of raw materials and commissions for production were directed by the merchants who sold the finished goods. Thus, Shi Sou may well have been the trade mark adopted by entrepreneur(s) who co-ordinated the work of a number of outworkers in the Jiangnan region during the late Ming period, ordering sets of items as trade demanded.

The same pattern may also apply to artefacts with Hu Wenming and other individual and family trademarks mentioned in this chapter. This idea may explain the lack of homogeneity in different works bearing the same mark, for example the two examples with signatures associated with Hu Wenming shown in this book.

Opposite page:

50   *Bronze brush stand, vase, ink cake stand and water-pot, inlaid with silver wire. Mark Shi sou,* 16th–17th century. Height of vase 10.5 cm. 5373-1901, M.605D-1924, M.605E-1924, 5410-1901.

51   The censer in Plates 51, 52 and 53 bears a Hu Wenming mark. It is dissimilar in both
52, 53 style and metal composition to the covered box by Zhu Chenming (a probable
associate of Hu Wenming) in Plate 42.

The censer is made from unalloyed copper of high purity which was cast and then finished using punching and engraving tools for fine detail. One of the three feet is a replacement, while the other two seem from their composition to have been made separately from a different batch of copper and then soldered on. The base plate was also soldered in. These elaborate methods were necessary to produce a piece whose landscape design is so beautifully detailed. Its conventions of representation, particularly the way stones are modelled and the manner in which a circular scene is joined by nebulous areas of rock and drifting cloud, resemble those of seventeenth century 'transitional' porcelain.

Continuing with recorded names, we learn that Anhui province was the home of Xie Qian, who was said to have cast bronze censers there in the 1640s and 1650s. Tang Peng cast iron picture panels at Wuhu during the Qianlong period (1736-95). Jiangxi province was where Zeng Ding worked, manufacturing gold seals at Taihe in the early Ming dynasty. Jiangxi was also famous for its mirror-making cities of Raozhou and Ji'an (see Chapter 7).

The city of Huzhou in Zhejiang province was famous for its families of mirror-makers, the Shi and Xue families (see Chapter 7). Pan Tie, mentioned by Gao Lian in his book *Zun sheng ba jian* (1591) was another native of Zhejiang. Jiaxing in northern Zhejiang was the place where Zhang Mingqi and Wang Fengjiang made bronze censers, the latter casting his name in sealscript upon them. The Ming pewterer Gui Maode also worked at Jiaxing, as did Huang Yuanji, active during the Ming/Qing transition, whose pewter vases were so good that they looked like silver. In the early Qing dynasty Shen Cunzhou was continuing the pewter-working tradition at Jiaxing.

During the Qing dynasty a few references are made to metal-workers from the north. Liu Xueshi, active during the Xianfeng reign (1851-61), cast bronze censers at Weixian in Shandong province. Weixian was also a place where impressed bronze buttons were made, by Xu Lun and Xu Boyuan among others. Shi Mou stamped out iron buttons at Wuchang in Hubei province.

It can be seen that the list of names given above is only a partial one, whose weight is distributed unevenly by the outpouring of 'literatures of connoisseurship' in the late Ming period. For this reason by far the greater number of artisans known to us by name came from the Jiangnan region and worked between the years 1550 and 1650. No work known to this author has yet been done to suggest what sort of living such craftsmen made. However, the fact that so many names of bronze- and pewter-workers are written down suggests that the craft of metal-working was held in relatively high esteem in the Ming and Qing dynasties.[99] In spite of this, very few surviving bronzes bear signatures and the range of signatures that does occur is narrow. Most of the names mentioned above are known to us solely through the literary record; it may be that future research will round out the picture somewhat more fully.

51-3 *Copper censer*, mark of Hu Wenming,
16th–17th century, diameter 9.5 cm,
M.2699-1931.

Fakes and Forgeries

The people who collected ancient bronzes during the Song, Yuan, Ming and Qing periods did not simply regard them as pretty ornaments. Old vessels, particularly those which had been buried for a long period, were held to possess special qualities of smell, of sound, and even of supernatural power over evil spirits. They were treasured as flower containers for similar reasons:

> I have heard it said that bronzes that have been in the soil a long time are deeply impregnated with the essence of the earth, and that this will maintain the beauty of flowers in their freshness and brightness. Buds will open out more quickly and will wither more slowly. This nurturing strength comes from the vase itself.[100]

These marvellous characteristics, coupled with the antiques' perceived beauty and rarity, made them highly desirable items. A thriving market for the buying and selling of ancient bronzes existed and naturally enough new bronzes were extensively faked to simulate old ones.

Qualities that were looked for as typifying old pieces included the type of script used to cast inscriptions, the way in which vessels and inscriptions were cast, and the quality of decor. By the Song period scholars were already assigning different forms of Chinese script to different dynasties (e.g. in the Zhou period they used large seal characters, in the Han regular script), and were also differentiating between intaglio and rilievo casting. Intaglio inscriptions, where the characters are below the surface of the surrounding bronze, were rightly held to be easier to cast than rilievo, where the design stands proud. From this it was deduced that intaglio casting was the earlier method of creating inscriptions. Later writers held that the very number of characters used indicated period, a view which has not been borne out by modern excavation:

> As regards inscriptions on various bronze vessels, those of the Xia, Shang and Zhou range from only one or two characters to no more than twenty or thirty. Those with two to three hundred characters definitely belong to the late Zhou or Qin dynasties.[101]

As to the quality of the decoration, it was generally held that the finer the work, the earlier the bronze. The equation that fine quality equals early date is a convenience that has been used by writers of many ages and in many places.

Those writers who mentioned the construction of bronze vessels assumed that archaic pieces were cast using the lost-wax method which was usual in their own time, another judgement which experience has shown to be false. The lost-wax method of casting bronzes started by making an inner core model. This inner mould was then coated with wax to the same thickness as was required of the

54 *Bronze vase inlaid with silver wire,*
copying an archaic vessel. The surface is
artificially patinated, and coloured
surface accretions can be seen. 16th–17th
century. Height 11 cm, 190–1899.

finished bronze. The soft wax was carved and worked with patterns and subsequently covered with several more layers of clay or some other suitable substance to form an outer mould. The whole thing was then baked to harden the inner and outer moulds and at this point the wax melted and flowed out. Molten bronze could then be poured into the gap between the inner and outer moulds, thus forming the finished product. Detailed patterns could be reproduced in soft wax and very complicated pieces could be made in several different moulds and then joined together.

The lost-wax method of casting was flexible and capable of achieving sophisticated results. It was different to the piece-mould method which had been used during China's bronze age. In the piece-mould method, the outer mould was constructed in several sections around a prototype model of the finished bronze (made in some material like clay). The patterns from this prototype were thus reproduced in reverse on the mould sections which then had to be assembled around a solid core with a space left between the two to receive the molten bronze. The outer mould sections had to be created and assembled in sections each time a bronze was cast. It was natural that later bronze-casters should prefer the lost-wax method and that contemporary commentators should assume that this method had always been used. In other matters collectors were extremely sharp-eyed and quick to spot any surface peculiarities. For example, they cautioned against pieces that showed any traces of cutting or chiselling.

One of the most obvious aspects of a bronze is its surface colour. Several authors detail the ideal hierarchy of patination:

Bronze vessels that have been interred under the earth a thousand years
appear pure green the colour of kingfisher feathers . . . those that have been
immersed in water a thousand years are pure emerald in colour with a jade-
like lustre. Those that have not been immersed as long as a thousand years
are emerald green but lack the lustre . . . those that have been transmitted
down from antiquity, not under water or earth but through the hands of
men, have the colour of purple cloth and a red mottling like sand, which
protrudes when excessive, and looks like first-quality cinnabar. When boiled
in a pan of hot water the mottling becomes more pronounced.[102]

54 It is evident that the artificial patination of vessels was one of the forgers' primary aims. Several recipes exist for inducing the 'emerald greens' and 'cinnabar reds' that were so admired.[103] One such account, by the Ming connoisseur Gao Lian, tells us:

After casting, the occasional defect is rubbed down, and where designs have
not cast clearly they are cut with tools. Then the vessel is soaked for a while
in a mixture of mud and fresh well water. Then it is put in an oven and baked
three times over, and next a solution of metallic salts (including sal-
ammoniac, alum, borax and sulphuric acid) is applied. The mixture is
painted over the vessel two or three times using a brush. After a couple of
days the mixture is washed off, then the vessel is dried, then rinsed and dried
again three or four times. Then a pit is dug and lined with red-hot charcoal,
vinegar is splashed all over the pit, the bronze is placed in the pit and soaked

in vinegar once more and covered with soil. After three days the bronze is taken out, and by this time has acquired a variety of patches of ancient-looking colour . . . To add other details to the surface . . . clear-gum resin . . . mixed with melted white wax is used. For blue-green patination a painter's pigment [azurite?] is used, for green malachite, and for red cinnabar . . . Small piles of salt, metal filings and cinnabar are used to cause coloured protrusions from the surface. A mixture of mercury and tin produces a silvery colour . . . which when covered with wax is dulled enough to fool the amateur. When rubbed in the hands a stink comes off the vessel that doesn't disappear completely even after washing. Sometimes when the forgers have completed this whole process they bury the vessel in acidic soil for a couple of years to give it a really ancient look.[104]

Gao's account appears to be first-hand, and may be presumed to be reasonably accurate. While it is not possible to check on the long process of cooking, soaking

55 *The Bushell Bowl*, bronze inlaid with gold and silver and with copper rim. Width 84.5 cm, 174-1899.

71

and burying he describes, the surface accretions mentioned do tally with those observed on actual bronzes. Considerable amounts of mercury were recorded on the surface of several pieces, suggesting that mercury compounds like cinnabar (red mercuric sulphide) were used. The duck censer in Plates 4 and 5 has heavily incrusted patination that even includes a large flake of malachite glued to the surface of the foot.

4, 5

Many later bronzes had shapes and decorations derived from ancient vessels. An important question is, which of them were forgeries intended to deceive? On the one hand, pieces were made to imitate but not to deceive in the same way as certain Chinese ceramic pieces did. For example, the dated Song vase (Pls. 31, 32, 46 and 47) bears patterns that hark back to archaic designs while at the same time displaying contemporary features. It was made for use as a temple flower vase and not as an 'antique'. On the other hand, old bronzes were being faked to deceive collectors at least as early as the Song dynasty. Some examples, like the inlaid bronzes described in Chapter 3 are known to have deceived collectors.

Therefore, in this chapter we shall concentrate on some of the more obvious 'fakes' in the V&A's collection. One of the bronze items that aroused controversy in this country at the beginning of the century is a large bronze basin, inlaid with gold and silver, and carved inside with a lengthy inscription. The acrimony surrounding the dating of this piece can be deduced from contemporary correspondence.

On 13 April 1909, a sinologist called Edward Harper Parker wrote to the Victoria and Albert Museum in portentous terms:

> Practically the whole world will enquire into the bowl affair & I will send
> results so soon as replies are complete.

By May of the same year his enquiries were still not complete, for he admonishes the hapless curators:

> This business is more important than perhaps you contemplate. I intend to
> have the Regent of China and all the Manchu princes closely cross-
> examined, not to mention the leading literary statesmen of China.

The Museum authorities privately protested at this excess of authority, but seem to have been powerless to stem a fierce debate that had raged in specialist journals since 1904.[105]

The bronze was bought in Peking in 1870 by S. W. Bushell, who was physician to the Legation there and an authority on several aspects of Chinese art.[106] It was sold to the Museum in 1899 for £80. Bushell had acquired the bronze from the collection of the Princes of Yi, collateral relatives of the Qing emperors. The inscription mentions a date of 590 BC and Bushell and his supporters stoutly defended this early attribution. However, mistrustful French sinologists had already condemned it by 1905 as 'faux', 'pas authentique' and 'suspect'. They were not the earliest detractors; two Chinese writers of the late 1700s, Feng Hao and Niu Shuyu, had already condemned what they called the *Jin Hou pan* (sacrificial bowl of the Marquis of Jin) as spurious on literary grounds.[107]

In truth, to the modern eye the chief speciality of the bowl is its immense size, which necessitated prodigious feats of casting; analysis of the vessel revealed that the piece had been made in vertical segments and that the composition of each segment was different. Indeed, such was the variation in components that it seems very likely that some of the metal used to create this huge vessel was melted-down scrap. The rim is pure copper. The shape is post-archaic while the inlaid gold and silver *taotie* (monster-masks) recall smaller Song and Ming examples. What we must remember is that the argument of both Chinese and Western experts revolved around the inscription.

Both the shape and the inscription of the 'Bushell bowl' were inspired by pieces like the *San shi pan* (sacrificial bowl of the San family), a magnificent basin on a high foot measuring 20.6 cm across and with a 357-character inscription. The San family bowl dates to about 800 BC, and Bushell mentions it as belonging to the Xu family at Yangzhou; it is now in the National Palace Museum in Taiwan.[108] Unlike the Bushell bowl, the San family bowl has chaste cast ornament without inlay and an inscription recording territorial boundaries and habitation.

56   The Bushell bowl is more ambitious. Its 538-character inscription is taken from the historical work *Zuo zhuan* ('Zuo Commentary'), compiled somewhere between 350 and 180 BC, thus post-dating a 590 BC attribution. A bronze inscription taken from the *Zuo zhuan* is unique, no other examples being known in China. Moreover, the inscribers have made several unfortunate mistakes. While some of the characters are copied from archaic vessels like the San family bowl others are entirely made up. Some of the characters imitate those found on stone drums of the period 770–470 BC, while yet others are taken from much later woodblock prints. Some characters are even written differently in two places on the vessel![109]

It seems likely that so complex a forgery was prepared for a learned Chinese collector, but as the characters are cut and not cast into the metal the bowl itself need not necessarily be party to the deception. At all events, after the characters were incised the whole inside surface of the bowl was artificially patinated, giving a lacquer-like appearance of age. The 'traces of beaten gold overlay' that Bushell reported with such excitement are merely shiny scratches made in the surface of the brassy metal by his exploratory knife.

Another category of bronzes that was much copied were those inlaid with precious metals. Magnificent early examples dating to the late Zhou and Han dynasties (sixth century BC to second century AD) were much admired by connoisseurs, and were extensively imitated in later times as pieces illustrated in this book show. An interesting variant on this practice was the use of parts of genuine early pieces which were combined with newer components to form showy composite vessels. The Ming writer Gao Lian describes his discovery of such forgeries:

> There are instances where broken fragments of genuine ancient vessels are put together in a new construction . . . When I was in the capital I saw two vessels like this. One called the *Zi fu ding* was small and serviceable, and everyone liked the way its decoration was arranged. It was faked by taking the lid of an archaic *hu* as the belly, patching together fragments of smashed vessels from old tombs above it, and using the handles of an ancient *ding* for handles, to make the whole thing into a censer *(lu)*. The second piece was a square vessel called the *Ya hu fu ding*, which was covered inside and out with mercury so that there was not a trace of decay anywhere. When first assessing its value I put it at a hundred gold pieces. It was about five inches square and serviceable, and everyone was fighting to buy it. But then when I examined it a second and third time I discovered it was made from the broken sherds of a square mercury-coated mirror which had been made into square pieces and cold-soldered together to form the four sides. The ears and legs from a damaged censer completed what could be called a really skilful job . . .[110]

The Victoria and Albert Museum collection contains several impressive composite vessels. The piece in Plate 57 is called a 'champion's vase', a verbal pun on the words *ying xiong* 'falcon and bear', the two creatures that are supposed to decorate such vases. In fact, the creatures appear to be a phoenix and a feline and the name 'champion's vase' is probably a fairly recent one. During the Ming dynasty (1368-1644) one author referred to such pieces as nuptial cups, but this was also inaccurate. Quite a number of vessels in this form are known, and although their exact function is unclear, their origin appears to date back at least as far as the Western Han dynasty (206 BC-AD 8).[111]

The vase in Plate 57 was made from seven or more pieces, the metal of the tubes being quite different from the other parts. The two tubes are inlaid with sheet silver and gold in a pattern of graceful spirals. Outlining some of the spirals is a series of broken, undulating, thin gold strips which look like flames. Between the spirals are tucked tiny figures of deer, birds, and two-legged creatures with beast heads which

58 *Bronze vessel and lid (dou) inlaid with gold.*
Composed of older lid with added
handle and base. Height 20 cm,
M.978-1928.

Left:
66 *Bronze figure of Li Tieguai,* Ming dynasty (1368–1644), height 22.5 cm, 68–1899.

Right:
67 *Bronze figure of Kui Xing* with wood stand, Ming dynasty (1368–1644), height 23.5 cm, Florence Bequest, M.211–1917.

suitable figures for women to pray to; many of Guanyin's reputed powers, for example her ability to 'send sons', are specifically concerned with women's issues. The Guanyin in Plate 69 holds a scroll, her right hand raised in a graceful *mudra* or mystic hand gesture, probably the *vitarka mudra* of argument. The decorated borders of her silk robe have been painstakingly reproduced in bronze.

The magnificent figures in Plates 70 and 71 are both Luohans, or disciples of the Buddha. In many Buddhist temples in China, along the east and west walls of the principal hall, are rows of seated Luohans. These disciples can number five hundred, but are usually depicted in temples in groups of either sixteen or eighteen, each with his own distinctive appearance and name. Many of the Luohans have strongly characterised faces suggesting that some may have been portraits taken

70 *Gilt bronze figure of the Luohan Gopaka,* 15th century, height 50 cm, FE.104-1970.

Opposite page:
71 *Gilt bronze figure of a Luohan,* 15th–17th century, height 26.7 cm, A.7-1967.

70 from life. The seated figure in Plate 70 is the Luohan Gopaka, and an inscription on the back in Chinese tells us that he was positioned as 'number seven on the east' in a Buddhist hall. Other similar figures are known, some possibly even coming from the same set, and a date in the fifteenth century is generally agreed for them. This Luohan is dressed in monk's robes whose embroidered borders are typically Ming dynasty in style. The front and back of his seat both bear inscriptions in Tibetan, as do the Buddhist sutras which he holds in his hands. His bronze body is lavishly gilded but his sides are undecorated and his back ungilt, suggesting that he was made to be viewed strictly from the front.

71 The Luohan in Plate 71 is a minor masterpiece of the sculptor's art. Seated at prayer with one knee drawn up, the contours of his body and face are strongly modelled. Much of the detail, like eyes, ears, tongue, toenails, folds in the robe and veins in the arms, is very carefully observed. Examination showed that the figure was cast using the lost-wax method and that a lot of the mould material together with the remnants of wires or chaplets remains in the hollow interior. There is a suggestion from the appearance of the mould material that iron might have been used to strengthen the core. The metal composition of the figure was shown to be

72 *Bronze figure of a Buddhist lion, parcel-gilt, with inlays,* 15th-16th century, length 9 cm, Salting Bequest, M.741-1910.

88

an alloy of copper with zinc and tin, and containing a small amount of lead. Even though it was not possible to determine whether the alloy had been made using metallic zinc, the presence of zinc suggests a date in the middle to second half of the Ming dynasty. The lead might have been used to improve the fluidity of the molten metal for it would not have seriously affected the colour or properties of the alloy. The Luohan is extensively gilded, and qualitative results showed mercury, gold and a tiny amount of silver, suggesting that fire-gilding was used and that there must have been a little silver in the gold. There is much less detail in the back of the figure which is only partly finished, presumably again because the Luohan was made to be viewed from the front.

The figures illustrated so far in this chapter were all made for the solemn purposes of burial or ritual display. There are a number of small bronze animal models, however, which were made as trinkets or for some useful purpose such as paper or scroll weights. In this way they are comparable to jade figures, and indeed examples like the Buddhist lions in Plates 72 and 73 are very similar to jade carvings.[119]

72   The lion in Plate 72 has the same flattened ears, snub triangular nose, bulging eyes, knobbed spine and flamelike ribbons along the thigh and shoulder as jade examples. It is also modelled in the round, with paws and tail reproduced in every detail underneath. Partly gilded and inlaid with semi-precious stones, it is a charming and endearing piece.

73   The sprightly beast in Plate 73, although rather different in style, is probably of similar Ming dynasty date.[120] It is only finished in a rather perfunctory manner underneath, but is decorated with gold flames on shoulder and hip and inlaid elsewhere with gold and silver.

73 *Bronze figure of a Buddhist lion inlaid with gold and silver,* 15th-16th century, length 9 cm, 182-1879.

Mirrors

Most Chinese mirrors in museum displays are shown face down, so that one views the decorated back and not the smooth reflecting surface. They are made of polished metal because the Chinese never developed forms of coated, reflective glass to use as mirrors. Although excavations in China have yielded a small number of lead-silica and lead-barium-silica glass objects dating back to about 500 BC, the glass industry really only developed in the early twentieth century.[121]

Among the metals the best reflector was silver, but this was expensive, so a high-tin copper alloy like speculum metal was often used instead. Such alloys had a silvery appearance when freshly cast and when in an uncorroded state. The reflecting surface could then be treated in various ways, to throw back a clearer image. If the tin content was around 30% polishing alone would suffice. If the tin content was less the surface could be 'silvered', i.e. treated with mercury or a copper/mercury amalgam. The latter is malleable and silvery in colour, sets hard, and can be polished and retains its lustre well in air. Zhao Xigu, writing in the thirteenth century, tells us:

> The faking of an ancient bronze is achieved by an application of mercury
> mixed with powdered tin, which is the preparation used at the present time
> to coat mirrors.[122]

Metal mirrors, particularly those with a lower tin content, needed to be repolished at regular intervals. If they were not maintained the surface became darkened and dulled, like the present appearance of the mirrors illustrated in this book. An idea of how frequently mirrors required treatment is given in the popular late Ming novel *Jin ping mei* ('The Golden Lotus'). In one chapter of this book great excitement is caused in the hero's household by the arrival of an itinerant mirror-polisher.[123] The heroine exclaims that her mirror is so worn that for the last two days it has been impossible to see anything clearly in it. A collection of large and small octagonal mirrors and a rectangular dressing-mirror are presented to the mirror-polisher. Fixing them on to his portable work-stool he 'uses mercury' to refurbish them, and in a very short time has them bright and shining new again. The young ladies are then able to admire their reflections which are 'as clear as an autumn pool', rather an apt description for the dark, flattering image that a polished metal mirror would throw back.

The tool used by such a mirror-polisher could well have been made of fired pottery, like that excavated from a thirteenth century tomb in southwest China. This example was a thin disc 26 cm in diameter, with three circular grooves on the back which may have been used to secure it to a workbench. Its grinding surface was worn smooth through repeated use and bore traces of blackish powder and

75 *Three bronze mirrors,* Song dynasty (960-1279), diameter 17 cm. M.78-1937, M.526-1910, M.62-1928.

Opposite page:

90

silver smears from the polishing process.[124]

The plain surfaces on most of the mirrors in this book have tarnished so that few give back any sort of reflection. However, it is not the undecorated, useful side of the mirrors with which we are concerned but the decorated back surfaces. It is from the designs and inscriptions on the back of mirrors that identification is arrived at.

The first Chinese mirrors appeared in the Shang dynasty (about 1700-1027 BC). Some of the finest mirrors were cast in the later Zhou and Han periods (about 500 BC-AD 220) and it was to the patterns of these times that later mirror-makers returned again and again. Early mirrors took the form of thin discs with a loop on the centre of the back for attaching the cord which served to hold them. The design of this loop or knob was often commented on by connoisseurs; Cao Zhao (1388) says of Tang dynasty (618-906) mirrors:

> They have particularly high, large knobs, and are therefore nicknamed
> 'Tang Big Noses'.

Not surprisingly, Tang mirrors were also imitated in later periods. Gao Lian (1591) talks of a contemporary craftsman Mr Pan [Pan Tie] who made mirrors with 'noses' and shell and wave patterns, and of craftsmen in Suzhou who made miniature imitation Han dynasty mirrors complete with patina.[125]

74   Plate 74 shows later mirrors in the styles of both the Han and Tang dynasties. The top mirror follows a Han dynasty (206 BC-AD 220) style, although the simplification of motif, pronounced broadening of the rim, and metal composition all point to a later date. Analysis revealed that this piece was one of a group of mirrors made of a metal alloy that had a small but definable zinc content.[126] The mirror on the left imitates a Tang dynasty (618-906) prototype, but the beaded band in the centre and the style in which the lions are rendered indicate a later period. Chinese scholarship suggests a Song dynasty (960-1279) attribution for the two, which are illustrated together with a mirror whose pattern and lobed border fall solidly within the Song tradition, showing no attempt at archaism. Its back surface has a raised design of paired mandarin ducks on a lotus pond while the reflecting surface had a concentration of mercury when analysed, indicating that the relatively low-tin, high-lead metal had originally been treated to improve its colour and reflecting properties.

Because of their use as a reflecting surface, mirrors have a different composition to other bronze vessels. The most common type of mirror, namely that made of a traditional alloy of copper, tin and lead, included some with as much as 30% tin. This speculum metal (still used in the modern world for the manufacture of telescope mirrors), is a difficult metal to work with because it is comparatively brittle. It could only be used for castings which did not need to be heavily worked in their final finishing. Mirrors made of this sort of alloy, however, would give a good reflecting surface when polished. A description of the casting of such mirrors is provided by a technological handbook published in 1637, which says:

> The mould used for casting mirrors is made of ash and sand, and the bronze
> is an alloy of copper and tin (zinc is not used). It is stated (elsewhere) that 'the
> mixture of the same amounts of copper and tin is called mirror-grade

74 *Three bronze mirrors,* Song dynasty
(960-1279), diameters 10 cm, 11 cm,
9 cm. M.67-1928, 201-1899, Hildburgh
Bequest M.286-1956.

bronze'. Its surface shines when a coating of mercury is applied; bronze itself
cannot be so bright.[127]

75 Three identical mirrors are shown in Plate 75. They bear a design of a small boat
sailing through choppy seas and the characters *huang ji chang tian* 'flashing brilliantly
up to the skies' presumably referring to the superior quality of the shiny mirror
when new. One of the three (M.526-1910) was actually excavated from a grave in
Korea from which several comparable pieces were recovered. Mirrors with this
pattern on them have been exhibited and published as Korean, but this very design
also appears on Song dynasty mirrors in China.[128] All three of the mirrors shown
are corroded in different ways, giving them different appearances. Although the
corrosion is substantial, making analysis of components difficult, it was possible to
determine that all three were rather similar in composition, being high-tin copper
alloys containing some lead. The excavated mirror also showed signs of a woven
textile pattern indicating that it may have been wrapped in a cloth when buried.

The edges of mirrors were often thickened. Their decoration was sometimes archaistic like the examples just shown, but otherwise echoed the designs found on contemporary crafts. They often bore images of daily life or popular stories for, unlike altar vessels and connoisseurs' pieces, mirrors were humble artefacts, made 76 for ordinary people. The example in Plate 76 is decorated with a story that was popular from the Song dynasty onwards. It shows the Tang dynasty Emperor Xuanzong (reigned 712-756), a Taoist initiate, on his fabled excursion to the moon. The emperor is said to have dreamed that he journeyed to the moon where he was entertained by fairy beings. He is seen crossing a bridge to where the moon goddess Chang E awaits him with her handmaidens, on a bank of clouds. To the right of the scene is a hare, another animal associated with the moon, standing beneath a cassia tree and pounding magic fungus in a pestle and mortar. In the foreground is a dragon among waves, a creature associated both with water and with emperors.

Another version of the Emperor Xuanzong's moon visit occurs on the back of 77 the foliated mirror at the bottom of Plate 77. The fan-shaped mirror above it bears a simpler scene of two gentlemen and their servant on a garden bridge overshadowed by a willow tree.

Below left:
76 *Bronze mirror*, Song dynasty (960-1279), diameter 21.5 cm, M.74-1937.

Below:
77 *Two bronze mirrors*, Song dynasty (960-1279), height 11.5 cm and diameter 17.3 cm, Wellcome Trust Gift, FE.84,FE.83-1982.

94

78   The mirrors in Plate 78 are decorated with processions of young boys surrounded by auspicious items; the larger mirror has two Taoist motifs associated with long life at the top, a crane and Shou Xing, star-god of longevity. Similar motifs are common on carved lacquer and porcelain during the Ming dynasty, particularly from the sixteenth century onwards.[129]

79   On the left of Plate 79 is a mirror showing two figures with conch shell and lotus leaf, both associated with Buddhism and emblematic of general good fortune. This piece is made of an alloy with low tin content, its reflecting side again being silver-coloured on account of the mercury used to improve its reflective surface. It bears the characters *qing xian* 'at leisure', a clever pun as the character *qing* meaning 'clear' suggests the good reflecting powers of the mirror, while the whole phrase subtly conveys the agreeable, leisured atmosphere in which such a mirror might be used. Firms which made mirrors were evidently skilled at marketing their products. The mirror on the right is decorated with two Chinese female figures but has an inscription in Tibetan *lantsha* characters, indicating that it may have been made in

78   *Two bronze mirrors*, Ming dynasty (1368-1644), diameters 15 cm and 8.6 cm. Hildburgh Bequest, M.275-1956, Macnaghten Bequest, M.4-1970.

95

79 *Two bronze mirrors,* Ming dynasty (1368-1644) and Yuan dynasty (1280-1368), diameters 7.3 cm, 8.5 cm. Wellcome Trust Gift, FE.86-1982, Hildburgh Bequest, M.285-1956.

China for the Tibetan market. There was a considerable trade in metal-work between China and Tibet between about 1300 and 1900.

Most excavated graves yield at least one mirror, which is often abraded, suggesting either long use or a cheap recasting. Excavated mirrors among the V&A's collection include the delicately-patterned pieces shown in Plates 80 and 81, whose surface patination indicates burial and whose designs can be matched with Liao and Song dynasty pieces unearthed in China.[130]

The mirror with handle in Plate 81 has a square panel on its back inscribed *Huzhou Shi Shiwulang zhen lian zhaozi,* 'genuine reflecting mirror by Shi Shiwulang of Huzhou'. The Shi family had a flourishing mirror-casting business at Huzhou in northern Zhejiang province, during the Southern Song dynasty (1127-1278). More than twenty different members of the Shi clan are known from their inscriptions on mirrors, and Shi Shiwulang's name is quite common.[131] Shi mirrors, which came in various shapes but were generally plain apart from their marks, were exported to both Korea and Japan and had a technical influence on Ming dynasty mirror-casting.

Huzhou continued its mirror-making activities during the Ming (1368-1644) and Qing (1644-1911) periods. During the Qing period the Xue family were renowned for their mirrors. The best-known member of the family was Xue Huigong, active during the Qianlong reign period (1736-95).[132] Two square mirrors in Plate 82 are signed with his given name, Xue Jinhou. They bear Taoistical formulas:

Upright, regular and brilliant; ten thousand *li* without dust; the waters and the heavens are all as one; penetrating deeply and understanding the myriad relationships.

The seals read 'Huzhou' and 'Made by Xue Jinhou'.[133] The larger mirror is said to have been picked up at the site of the Ming tombs in Nanking in 1920. The background colour of the smaller one is not dirt but colouring applied to contrast against the raised characters. The colour was derived from the sap of a tree, *Pinus massoniana,* a native of southeast China.[134]

80, 81

82

80 *Two bronze mirrors,* Liao dynasty (907–1125) and Song dynasty (960–1279), diameters 13 cm and 10 cm. Cockell Gift, M.31–1939, M.85–1937.

81 *Two bronze mirrors,* Liao dynasty (907–1125) and Song dynasty (960–1279), diameter 11 cm and length 17 cm. M.90–1920, Pope-Hennessy Gift, M.312–1921.

82 *Two bronze mirrors,* Qianlong reign period (1736–95), diameters 9.1 cm and 9.5 cm. Wellcome Trust Gift, FE.87-1982, Sennane Gift, M.107-1920.

83 Another magnificent Taoist mirror appears in Plate 83. The metal composition is an alloy with high tin content. The back surface shows the Animals of the Four Quarters in the centre (dragon, phoenix, tiger, tortoise), with the twelve animals of the Chinese zodiac cycle among grape vines encircling them, followed by bands containing the Eight Trigrams, star constellations and a long inscription. This reads:

> This mirror is made of the essence of *chang geng* [the 'evening star', probably Venus] and *bai hu* ['white fox', a constellation, probably Sirius],
> light and heat united in making the mirror, from the mountains and rivers came its metals,
> it was made after the sphere of the heavens and the essence of the earth,
> placed upon it are the Eight Trigrams,
> in fashioning this mirror I have been dependent on the five elements,
> the hundred animals will be reflected without error, nor can the ten thousand things escape their reflections,
> the possession of this mirror will be a precious thing, for wealth and official position will come to the owner without asking.[135]

It is evident, even from the small selection described here, that many mirrors had associations with the Chinese mystical philosophy of Taoism. Some mirrors were produced not for cosmetic purposes but to be held in the hand of Taoist monks when they performed their ceremonial rites. Such mirrors, like those illustrated in Plates 82 and 83, had suitable inscriptions and often bore the Eight Trigrams *(ba gua)*.

Ordinary mirrors, because of their reflecting properties, have legendary power to ward off evil spirits and thus can also be linked to Taoist beliefs. Seeing their own hideous appearance demons are believed to be frightened away. Some people in country districts of China still keep mirrors beneath the roof ridge in the eaves of their houses, or on the outside of their doors, or just inside the doors, so that these

83 *Bronze mirror,* Song dynasty (960–1279), diameter 27 cm, Hildburgh Bequest, M.296–1956.

principal routes of entry into the home are protected. Such beliefs have ancient origins; during the Ming dynasty (1644–1911) mirrors were suspended above temple and domestic altars while during the Han dynasty (206 BC–AD 220) some corpses were buried with a mirror placed on top of their faces to ward off malignant spirits.

84   The mirror in Plate 84 has a cartouche inscribed *Ji'an lu Hu Dongyou zuo,* 'made by Hu Dongyou of Ji'an district'. A very similar mirror, excavated at Jiujiang in Jiangxi province, has been dated with some precision to the mid-Yuan dynasty, around 1310–20. From the Song dynasty onwards Ji'an and Raozhou, both in Jiangxi province, were two of the most famous mirror-making cities in China. A number of mirrors with inscriptions linking them to Ji'an are known, the whole group being characterised by thin bodies, sketchy patterns, and tendency to copy Han dynasty (206 BC–AD 220) designs.[136]

漢雲龍鑑

85   An early Ming mirror is shown in Plate 85. The design is of a five-clawed scaly
        dragon writhing among clouds on a wavy background with a square cartouche
        containing the inscription: 'made on a day in the fifth month of the twenty-second
        year of Hongwu', that is 1390. A number of similar mirrors are recorded, and as
        there is nothing in either design nor metal composition to suggest a contrary
        opinion, we may conclude the dating to be accurate.[137] Two examples are kept in
        the Palace Museum in Taiwan,[138] and one of them was illustrated in Qianlong's
86   catalogue of Palace bronzes *Xi Qing gu jian.* The catalogue compilers failed to read
        the mirror's inscription fully and labelled it as dating to the Han dynasty (206 BC-
        AD 220).[139]

        By the late Ming period certain mirrors had become collectable items and the
        fastidious Wen Zhenheng provides an inevitable list of do's and don'ts concerning
        mirrors used by gentlemen:
            The best mirrors date to the Qin dynasty (221-206 BC), have inclined backs
            with a shiny patina like black lacquer, are thickly made, and have no
            patterns. Next best are mercury-coloured mirrors with archaic-style flowers

88 *Bronze mirror with handle,* 12th-14th century, length 16.2 cm, Hardcastle Gift, FE.230-1974.

102

on the back. The following are vulgar, and cannot be used: small, round mirrors with fussy patterns inlaid in gold and silver and with garish patina; lobed, octagonal or square mirrors with handles, that can be carried about as hand-mirrors.[140]

Wen's mention of hand-mirrors is significant, for many mirrors were intended to be mounted on stands and thus to form part of stationary dressing-tables. Paintings show ladies making-up before just such mounted mirrors. The bronze mirror stand in Plate 87 takes the form of a mythical single-horned animal called *xiniu*, and dates to the Song or Yuan dynasty.[141]

Two hand-mirrors with handles for carrying are shown in Plates 81 and 88. The example in Plate 88 shows another *xiniu* gazing up at the moon from an island in the waves, with behind him two fairy creatures bearing branches of magic fungus and coral.[142]

In conclusion, two later mirrors from the Museum's collection are shown, both made of brass. The eight-lobed mirror in Plate 89 is the only mirror identified as being a Beta-brass, i.e. with more than 40% zinc, a rather brittle alloy which would have been very yellow when new. It shows a 'fish-transforming-into-dragon', a lucky motif which encourages the overcoming of difficulties to achieve success.

89 *Brass mirror,* Qing dynasty (1644-1911), diameter 9 cm, Wellcome Trust Gift, FE.89-1982.

90   The large mirror in Plate 90 has lost its central soldered knob, and is decorated with a butterfly and flower design that recalls Qing dynasty porcelain and textiles. The four characters read *lin feng cheng xiang*, 'may the unicorn and phoenix bring you luck' (i.e. may you bear many sons), a fitting message for an object used by women.

It can be seen that although mirrors were small, mass-produced items much time and energy were devoted to their auspicious decoration.

90   *Brass mirror,* Qing dynasty (1644–1911), diameter 30.5 cm, 5458–1901.

Notes

1 A full internal report was compiled, reference 35/88.

2 Li Xueqin, *The Wonder of Chinese Bronzes* (Beijing, 1980), p. 28.

3 Recent excavations have yielded inscribed bamboo strips that add credence to the dating of the Annals. In 1972 two tombs dating to the reign of the Wudi Emperor of the Western Han period (140-135 BC) at Linyi in Shandong province yielded 4,900 strips. These were fragments from a book called *Sun zi bing fa* ('Master Sun's Art of War') and of a missing work *Sun Bin bing fa* (Sun Bin's Art of War). In 1975, 1,100 strips on law were found in a tomb dating to around 210 BC at Yunmeng in Hubei province.

4 See Li Xueqin, pp. 43-5.

5 Details of the major Song historical and geographical sources are provided in *A Sung Bibliography (Bibliographie des Sung)* initiated by Etienne Balazs, edited by Yves Hervouet (Hong Kong, 1978).

6 It must be stressed that available copies of these catalogues in the West are reprints of much later date, most of them not earlier than sixteenth century at best. It has been argued that successive reprints led to the re-cutting of printer's blocks and thus to a decline in the quality of illustrations. There is a further danger that unusual details may have been added in at later dates. Robert Poor, 'Notes on the Sung Dynasty Archaeological Catalogs', *Archives of the Chinese Art Society of America*, 19 (1965), 33-44, argues the authenticity of various versions of the texts in detail, and lists known editions of *Kao gu tu, Xu kao gu tu* and *Xuanhe bo gu tu lu*.

7 See Balazs and Hervouet, p. 200. Poor, pp. 34-8.

8 R. C. Rudolph, 'Preliminary Notes on Sung Archaeology', *The Journal of Asian Studies*, XXII, no. 2 (February 1962), 169-77 (pp. 170-1).

9 Quoted in Rudolph, p. 170.

10 Balazs and Hervouet, p. 201.

11 R. Soame Jenyns and William Watson, *Chinese Art: — The Minor Arts*, 2 vols. (London, 1965 and Oxford, 1981), I, p. 87.

12 The most complete refutation was provided by Paul Pelliot, 'Le pretendu album de porcelaines de Hiang Yuan-pien', *T'oung Pao* XXXII, (1936), 15-58. His arguments against authenticity include a detailed summary of the history of the book. The first person to mention a version of the text was a scholar called Hang Shijun (1696-1773), who in a collection of short articles published in 1776 describes a book called *Xuande yi qi pu* ('Catalogue of Ritual Vessels of the Xuande Period'), with no recorded illustrations. During the second half of the eighteenth century a manuscript bearing a slightly different title to that seen by Hang was presented to the editors of the massive compilation of rare books for the imperial library called the *Si ku quan shu* ('Complete Library in Four Branches of Literature'). That version was called *Xuande ding yi pu* ('Catalogue of Tripod Vessels of the Xuande Period'), was in eight chapters, and had a preface dated 1428 and a postscript dated 1534. The latter mentioned colour plates, but the manuscript was presented to the imperial editors without them. During the nineteenth century traces of a more complete recension in twenty chapters occurred, and then finally in 1928 a complete edition in twenty chapters with black and white illustrations appeared, the *Xuande yi qi tu pu*. This in itself was a collation of two manuscripts, one of which was said to have been found in a second-hand bookshop a few years before.

13 Wai-Kam Ho, 'Late Ming Literati: Their Social and Cultural Ambience', in *The Chinese Scholar's Studio — Artistic Life in the Late Ming Period*, edited by Chu-tsing Li and James C. Y. Watt (New York, 1987), 23-36 (p. 24).

14 Cheng Changxin and Zhang Xiande, 'Ming jinpian tonglu he cuojin lilu' ('A Ming Golden Bronze Censer and an Inlaid Tripod Censer'), *Wenwu* (1979.12), 84-5. See Rose Kerr, 'A Preliminary Note on Some Qing Bronze Types', *Oriental Art*, N.S.26 (1980.4), 447-56.

15 A list of the major works is provided by Li Xueqin, p. 28.

16 Thomas Lawton, 'An Imperial Legacy Revisited: Bronze Vessels from the Qing Palace Collection', *Asian Art*, 1, no. 1 (Fall/Winter 1987-8), 50-79.

17 Zhao Xigu, *Dong tian qing lu ji*, Meishu congshu, chu ji, di jiu ji (Shanghai, 1928), *juan* 4, pp. 10b-14b. See also Noel Barnard, 'The Incidence of Forgery Amongst Archaic Chinese Bronzes — Some Preliminary Notes', *Monumenta Serica*, XXVII, no. 7.

18 Zhao, p. 11b.

19 The easiest way to consult this work is in Sir Percival David's translation with commentary: *Chinese Connoisseurship — The Ko Ku Yao Lun — The Essential Criteria of Antiquities* (London, 1971), which also includes a facsimile of the Chinese text.

20 David, p. 11.

21 R. H. van Gulik, *Chinese Pictorial Art as Viewed by the Connoisseur* (Rome, 1958), p. 51.

22 Gao Lian, *Yan xian qing shang jian*, Meishu congshu, san ji, di shi ji (Shanghai, 1928), *juan* 2, pp. 13a-22a.

23 Gao, p. 18b.

24 Tu Long derived a comfortable living off Gao Lian, from whom ninety per cent of his text comes. It is interesting to observe this very direct example of plagiarism, a practice so common at the time.

25 Zhang Yingwen, *Qing bi cang*, Meishu congshu, chu ji, di ba ji (Shanghai, 1928), *juan shang*, p. 3a.

26 The accurate translation of the title is discussed by Craig Clunas, 'Human Figures in the Decoration of Ming Lacquer', *Oriental Art*, NS 32 (1986.2), 177-88 (p. 188).

27 van Gulik, p. 490.

28 Wen Zhenheng, *Zhang wu zhi jiao zhu*, revised edition with notes by Chen Zhi (Nanjing, 1984), *juan* 10, p. 352.

29 L. Vandermeersch, 'L'arrangement de fleurs en Chine', *Arts Asiatiques*, XI (1965.2), 79-140.

30 Vandermeersch, p. 94.

31 Vandermeersch, p. 94.

32 A complete translation was published by Penguin Books in 1983.

33 The title is taken from the position of Wang's study-cum-library which was to the north of a pool in the garden of his residence. Wang Shizhen, *Chi bei ou tan*, Zhonghua shuju (Beijing, 1980), p. 2.

34 The story was current by the seventeenth century, in such works as Liu Tong's 1635 *Di jing jing wu lüe* ('Summary of Sights and Events in the Imperial City'), but was already contested in the eighteenth. See Pelliot, p. 36.

35 Wang's assumed name (*hao*) was taken from the name of the garden room that the official, poet and literary critic Shen Deqian (1673-1769) used as a study in Suzhou. Wang Yingkui, *Liunan sui bi*, Zhonghua shuju (Beijing, 1983), p. 1.

36 Xie Kunpan, *Quan yu suo sui* (not the complete manuscript) in Meishu congshu, san ji, di ba ji (Shanghai, 1928), *juan shang*, p. 2b.

37 *Yuan ming yuan da mu zuo ding lie* ('Regulations for Making the Large Timbers of the Yuan Ming Yuan'), located in the Asian Division of the Library of Congress, Washington D.C. (B.182.25). See also Carroll B. Malone, 'Current Regulations for Building and Furnishing Chinese Imperial Palaces, 1727-1750', *Journal of the American Oriental Society*, 49 (1929), 234-43.

38 *Yuan ming yuan da mu zuo ding lie*, *juan* 24, pp. 1a-13a.

39 *Yuan ming yuan da mu zuo ding lie*, *juan* 25, p. 25b.

40 *Yuan ming yuan da mu zuo ding lie*, *juan* 36, p. 14b.

41 Wen, *juan* 10, p. 357.

42 The name *jue* was first given to the vessel by scholars during the Song dynasty and may thus not be an ancient term. Research done by the National Palace Museum in Taipei in connection with the 'Exhibition of Shang and Zhou Wine Vessels', publication forthcoming.

43 Liu Wei, from Ciqi in Zhejiang, *jinshi* (i.e. a successful candidate at the highest level in the imperial examination system) of 1439, has a biography in *Ming shi*, volume 15, *juan* 164, p. 4455. Guangdong was the last posting of his career. For Wu Zhong see *Ming Qing jinshi timing beilu suoyin*, volume 1, p. 860. There were three men of that name (same characters) in the fifteenth century. Only one came from Leping in Jiangxi, and he was *jinshi* of 1454.

44 Cao Zhao in *Gegu yaolun*, Gao Lian in *Zun sheng ba jian*, among others.

45 See *Nei Menggu chutu wenwu xuanji* ('A Selection of Artefacts Unearthed in Inner Mongolia'), edited by the Inner Mongolian Autonomous Region Archaeological Unit (Beijing, 1963), pp. 119-21.

46 See Rose Kerr, 'A Preliminary Note . . .', p. 452, where the piece was described as eighteenth century.

47 For a pattern of boys playing, in which the background and rocks are also treated in a similar way, see *Gu Gong bo wu yuan zang diao qi* ('Carved lacquer in the Collection of the Palace Museum'), commentary by Wang Shixiang and Zhu Jiajin (Peking, 1985), pls. 138, 139. For a similar dragon design see Wang Shixiang, *Ming shi jia ju zhen shang* ('The Golden Age of Chinese Furniture') (Hong Kong, 1985), 127, 201, 150.

48 Åke Setterwall, Stig Fogelmarck and Bo Gyllensvärd, *The Chinese Pavilion at Drottningholm* (Malmö, 1974), p. 199.

49 Joseph Needham and Lu Gwei-djen, *Science and Civilisation in China, Volume 5, Chemistry and Chemical Technology: Part II, Spagyrical Discovery and Invention: Magisteries of Gold and Immortality* (Cambridge, 1974), p. 219.

50 Sung Ying-hsing, *Tien-Kung K'ai-Wu: Chinese Technology in the Seventeenth*

Century, translated by E-Tu Zen Sun and Shiou-Chuan Sun (Pennsylvania, 1966), p. 247.

51   S. G. E. Bowman, M. Cowell, J. Cribb, 'Two Thousand Years of Coinage in China: An Analytical Survey', *Historical Metallurgy Society Journal* (forthcoming in 1989).

52   The evidence supplied by brass coins is supplemented by the 1637 description of brass manufacture using distilled zinc in *Tien-Kung K'ai-Wu*, see note 50.

53   A gold-splashed bronze censer with Chongzhen reign period mark (1628-44) is illustrated in *Chinese Antiquities from the Brian S. McElney Collections*, exhibition organised by the Hong Kong Museum of Art (Hong Kong, 1987), no. 135.

54   Jessica Rawson has noted the influence of both silver and bronze on ceramic form and decoration. She has published a number of papers on the subject, and expresses her views in the book *Chinese Ornament, The Lotus and the Dragon* (London, 1984).

55   A pear-shaped vase with loop handles was excavated from the Yuan dynasty tomb of Lady Ye, wife of Song Sheng, at Nanking. The best illustration of this piece is in Tsugio Mikami and The Zauho Press, *Sekai toji zenshu — Ceramic Art of the World, Volume 13, Liao, Chin and Yuan Dynasties* (Tokyo, 1981), p. 185.

56   CPAM, Sichuan, 'Sichuan Jianyang Dongxi Yuanyichang Yuan mu' ('Yuan Dynasty Tombs at Yuanyichang, in Dongxi, Jianyang, Sichuan'), *Wenwu* (1987.2), 70-87, pls. 2&3.

57   John Ayers, 'Blanc-de-Chine: Some Reflections', *Transactions of the Oriental Ceramic Society* (1986-1987), 13-36 (p. 23).

58   A Yongzheng period (1723-35) vase of identical form is illustrated in John Ayers and Masahiko Sato, *Sekai toji zenshu — Ceramic Art of the World, Volume 15, Ch'ing Dynasty* (Tokyo, 1983), pl. 40.

59   Rose Kerr, 'Metalwork and Song Design: A Bronze Vase Inscribed in 1173', *Oriental Art*, NS 32 (1986.2), 161-76.

60   *Wenwu* (1987.2), pp. 80, 83. See note 56.

61   A vase with identical design was recovered from a Jin dynasty hoard, *Kaogu* (1987.12), pp. 1142, 1143. This author had previously published the comparable V&A vessel as probably being of Yuan-early Ming dynasty date, see Rose Kerr, 'The Evolution of Bronze Style in the Jin, Yuan and Early Ming Dynasties', *Oriental Art*, NS 28 (1982.2), 146-58 (p. 157).

62   For the spiral pattern round the belly of the vase in Plate 35, see a vase from a Jin dynasty hoard in *Kaogu* (1987.12), p. 1143. For the pattern on the vase in Plate 36 see a censer from a Jin dynasty tomb in Shanxi, *Wenwu* (1978.4), p. 12. For the diaper pattern on the vase in Plate 37, see a Yuan dynasty vase excavated in Mongolia in *Nei Menggu chutu wenwu xuanji*, p. 121.

63   *Special Exhibition of Cultural Relics Found off Sinan Coast*, edited by the National Museum of Korea (Seoul, 1977). *Relics from the Seabed at Sinan*, edited by the Bureau of Culture Properties (Seoul, 1983).

64   E.g: *Kōro* ('Censers'), edited by the Nezu Bijutsukan, exhibition catalogue (Tokyo, 1972). 'Ikebana', edited by Ichirō Baba, *Taiyō ('The Sun')*, special issue (1975.12). *Art of the Tea Ceremony*, edited by the Tokyo National Museum, exhibition catalogue (Tokyo, 1980). *Hanaike* ('Flower Vases'), edited by the Tokugawa Bijutsukan and Nezu Bijutsukan, exhibition catalogue (Nagoya/Tokyo, 1982).

65   Samuel Bing, *Artistic America, Tiffany Glass, and Art Nouveau* (Paris, 1895), revised edition with an introduction by Robert Koch (Cambridge, Massachusetts, 1970), p. 1.

66   Joseph Needham and Wang Ling, *Science and Civilisation in China, Volume 4, Physics and Physical Technology: Part 1, Physics* (Cambridge, 1962), p. 328.

67   A similar iron *tou hu* with inscription dating it to the seventh year of the Wanli period (1579) was sold by Sotheby's in London on 29 October 1982, lot 156.

68   Watson and Jenyns, pp. 98-107.

69   The work was undertaken for Michael Goedhuis of Colnaghi Oriental Ltd. I am grateful to him for allowing me to quote these results. Two V&A pieces were tested separately, M.726-1910 and M.978-1928.

70   The goose vessel, owned by Michael Goedhuis, was thermoluminescence tested and gave a twelfth to thirteenth century date.

71   Thermoluminescence dating analysis was carried out by Doreen Stoneham, who points out that this method does not strictly speaking ever represent a complete dating because of the small samples obtained and because pieces are investigated out of their burial context.

72   A large collection of curio cabinets, complete with their contents is housed in the National Palace Museum in Taipei. This imperial collection survives almost intact, unlike the boxes and their contents belonging to lower-ranking gentlemen which must have become separated and dispersed. It is thought that the idea of curio cabinets (in Chinese *duo bao ge*) developed out of the sort of fitted travelling-cases and stationery-cases used by gentlemen during the Ming period.

73   The popularity of squared spiral patterns to decorate the necks of vessels is shown by some of the massive stone vessels at the Ming tombs near Beijing, which

copy bronzes. Ann Paludan, *The Imperial Ming Tombs* (New Haven and London, 1981), 50, 148. The vessels illustrated come from the tombs of the Emperors Zhengde (died 1521) and Wanli (died 1620).

74 Compare dragons on Ming furniture in Wang, *Ming shi jia ju zhen shang*, 131, 137, 162.

75 Gao, p. 14b.

76 See: Gerard Tsang and Hugh Moss, *Chinese Metalwork of the Hu Wenming Group*, catalogue at the International Asian Antiques Fair (Hong Kong, 1984).

77 The text was not actually published till the eighteenth century.

78 Wen, *juan* 7, p. 247.

79 Compare dragon form in *Zhongguo meishu quanji: gongyi meishu bian, 10, jin yin boli falang qi* ('The Complete Arts of China: The Applied Arts, 10, Gold, Silver, Glass and Enamels'), edited by Yang Boda (Beijing, 1986), p. 88.

80 *The Times Atlas of China* (London, 1974), *XXX*.

81 This and any of the following references to historical mining activities which appear without credits were derived from William F. Collins, *Mineral Enterprise in China* (Tientsin, 1922), pp. 13-32.

82 *The Times Atlas of China, XXX*.

83 The advance registered was that from 1090 coppery solution from some mines had begun to be treated with iron for the deposition of copper.

84 This piece is discussed in detail in an earlier article: see note 59.

85 Jerome Ch'en, 'Sung Bronzes — An Ecomonic Analysis', *Bulletin of the School of Oriental and African Studies*, 28 (1965), 613-26.

86 Robert Hartwell, 'The Evolution of the Early Northern Sung Monetary System, AD 960-1025', *Journal of the American Oriental Society*, 87 (1967), 280-9.

87 Shiba Yoshinobu, 'Commerce and Society in Sung China', translated by Mark Elvin, *Michigan Abstracts of Chinese and Japanese Works on Chinese History*, 2 (1970), p. 125.

88 *Chin P'ing Mei: The Adventurous History of Hsi Men and his Six Wives*, translated by Bernard Miall from the abridged version by Franz Kuhn (Bristol, 1939), p. 10.

89 Han-sheung Chuan and Lung-wah Lee, 'The Annual Expenditure of Silver Taels of the T'ai-ts'ang Vault after the Mid-Ming Period (A Summary)', *The Journal of The Institute of Chinese Studies of the Chinese University of Hong Kong*, 6 (1973.1), 169-244.

90 William S. Atwell, 'International Bullion Flows and the Chinese Economy *Circa* 1530-1650', *Past & Present*, 95 (1982), 68-90.

91 Han-sheung Chuan, 'The Overseas Trade of Macao after the Mid-Ming Period', *The Journal of The Institute of Chinese Studies of the Chinese University of Hong Kong*, 5 (1972.1), 245-71.

92 Atwell, p. 89.

93 Han-sheung Chuan, 'The Copper Mining Industry in Yunnan during the Ch'ing Period', *The Journal of the Institute of Chinese Studies of the Chinese University of Hong Kong*, 7 (1974.1), 155-82.

94 Collins, p. 34.

95 Yeh-chien Wang, 'The Secular Trend of Prices during the Ch'ing Period (1644-1911)', *The Journal of the Institute of Chinese Studies of the Chinese University of Hong Kong*, 5 (1972.2), 347-71.

96 Some of the artisans named here are mentioned in the texts discussed in

Chapter 1. Many more are listed by Zhou Nanquan, *'Ming Qing gong yi mei shu min jiang'* ('Named Artists and Craftsmen of the Ming and Qing') *Gugong bowuyuan yuankan* (1985.1), 83-96 (pp. 87-8).

97 See for example the Wanli period excavated and dated scholar's accoutrements in Li and Watt, 124-8, 180-4.

98 An interesting example is that of French medieval illustrated manuscript production, discussed by James Douglas Farquhar, *Creation and Imitation: The Work of a Fifteenth-Century Manuscript Illuminator* (Fort Lauderdale, Florida, 1976), pp. 41-3, and Rowan Watson, *The Playfair Hours: A Late Fifteenth Century Illuminated Manuscript from Rouen* (London, 1984), pp. 23-4.

99 Craig Clunas, 'Some Literary Evidence for Gold and Silver Vessels in the Ming Period (1368-1644)', in *Pots and Pans; A Colloquium on Precious Metals and Ceramics*, edited by Michael Vickers and Julian Raby, *Oxford Studies in Islamic Art*, 3 (1987), 83-7 (p. 84).

100 Yuan Hongdao writing in about 1605. His remarks are reproduced in several other books.

101 Liang Tongshu (1723-1815), *Gu tong qi kao* ('Examination of Ancient Bronze Vessels'), Meishu congshu chu ji, di san ji, p. 14a. Quoted in Barnard, p. 126.

102 Zhao, p. 10b.

103 Just how widespread the practice of faking old bronzes was is demonstrated by an anonymous text, *Ju jia bi yong shi lei* ('Categorised Affairs and Usages Necessary to the Householder'), published around 1600. This was no scholarly handbook on elegant living but rather an encyclopaedic tome for the *nouveau riche* on how to keep up social appearances. Under 'necessary items for the studio' it contains a recipe for giving bronzes an ancient colour, copying the words of Zhao Xigu, Cao Zhao, Gao

Lian *et al*, and a recipe for polishing them up afterwards. I am indebted to Craig Clunas for this reference, and to the notes he took from the text in Peking.

104 Gao Lian, p. 16b, a section entitled *xin zhu wei zao* ('New Counterfeit Castings'). Gao is expanding on accounts of artificial patination described in the Song dynasty by Zhao Xigu and in the Yuan by Cao Zhao. Gao's is the most complete of several Ming descriptions of the process.

105 The bowl was discussed by Chavannes, Pelliot, Giles and Vissiere (against its antiquity) and by Bushell, Parker and Hopkins (for). Edouard Chavannes, *T'oung-Pao* (March, 1905), p. 120. Paul Pelliot, *Bulletin de l'Ecole française de l'Extrême Orient*, (1905), p. 219. S. W. Bushell, *Chinese Art*, Victoria & Albert Museum Art Handbook, 2 vols (London, 1904-), I, 84-8, figs. 49, 50, (1909), 87-91, figs. 49, 50, (1924), 72-6, figs. 49, 50. E. H. Parker, 'The Ancient Chinese Bowl in the South Kensington Museum', *T'oung-Pao*, series II, (X.4). H. A. Giles, *Adversaria Sinica* (1911), 283-97. Vissiere, 1913.

106 See Rose Kerr, *Chinese Ceramics — Porcelain of the Qing Dynasty 1644-1911*, Victoria and Albert Museum Far Eastern Series (London, 1986), pp. 20, 29.

107 Barnard, p. 127, quoting Rong Geng.

108 National Palace Museum, *Ku Kung pao chi* ('Treasures of the Palace Museum') (Taipei, 1985), no. 24.

109 Verbal communications from Professor Li Xueqin, when he inspected the bowl on 28 February 1986.

110 Gao, p. 18b. See Barnard, p. 121.

111 James C. Y. Watt, *Chinese Jades from Han to Ch'ing*, The Asia Society (New York, 1980), 156-7. Watt illustrates a jade champion's vase that he attributes to the Song dynasty, twelfth-thirteenth centuries AD.

112 Examination carried out by Doreen Stoneham.

113 See *Wenwu cankao ziliao* (1957.5), p. 52, *Wenwu* (1959.2), p. 40, *Wenwu* (1982.6), p. 29, *Wenwu* (1985.6), p. 68, *Wenwu* (1987.7), p. 92.

114 *Wenwu* (1987.2), pp. 66-9, includes a report of a tomb datable to 1237.

115 The Tokugawa Art Museum, *The Shogun Age Exhibition* (Tokyo, 1983), p. 107.

116 See Stephen Little, *Realm of the Immortals: Daoism in the Arts of China*, The Cleveland Museum of Art (Cleveland, 1988), 10-13, 42.

117 Derek Gillman, 'Ming and Qing ivories: figure carving' in *Chinese Ivories from the Shang to the Qing*, The Oriental Ceramic Society (London, 1984), p. 100.

118 Gillman, p. 97.

119 Examples like the mythical animal illustrated in Ip Yee, *Chinese Jade Carving* (Hong Kong, 1983), no. 161, and Watt, *Chinese Jades . . .*, no. 54. Ip Yee dates such pieces to the Ming dynasty, and Watt more precisely to the late fifteenth- sixteenth century.

120 Compare an example in Li and Watt, *The Chinese Scholar's Studio . . .*, no. 65.

121 Zhang Fukang, lecture on *Chinese Glass* delivered at the School of Oriental and African Studies, University of London, on 10 November 1986.

122 Zhao, p. 12b.

123 *Fleur en Fiole d'Or (Jin Ping Mei cihua)* (Tours, 1985), translated by André Lévy, pp. 201-4. Cai Guoliang, *Jin ping mei kaozheng yu yanjiu* ('Investigation and Textual Research on the novel 'Jin ping mei' ') (Xi'an, 1984), pp. 197-8.

124 Sichuan Provincial Museum and Pengxian Institute, 'Nan Song Yu Gongzhu fufu he zangmu' ('The tomb of Yu Gongzhu and his wife of the Southern Song Dynasty'), *Kaogu xuebao* (1985.3), 383-402 (p. 398).

125 Gao, p. 18b.

126 Analysis showed that the mirrors in the V&A could be assigned to three main groups: A) copper alloys with a high tin content; the majority of mirrors came within this group which represents the typical composition of all early mirrors: B) copper alloys with a low tin content which were just like ordinary casting metal: C) copper/zinc alloys with variable zinc concentration. The mirror described in the text was a 'group B' type.

127 Sung Ying-Hsing, p. 165.

128 A mirror of this pattern is illustrated as Korean in the exhibition catalogue by Dr Youngsook Pak, *Korean Art 5th to 19th century. From European Museums and Collections* (Ingelheim am Rhein, 1984), p. 51. An identical mirror (not excavated) from Hubei is illustrated in *Wenwu* (1986.7), p. 88

129 For an identical mirror to M.4-1970 see *Baofeng wenhuaguan shoucang yi mian diaoke renwu jing* ('A Mirror with Relief Figure Decoration in the Baofeng Cultural Institute [Henan Province]'), *Kaogu yu wenwu* (1983.4), p. 13.

130 *Wenwu* (1956.12), p. 37, *Wenwu* (1973.8), 36-8, *Wenwu* (1984.3), 79-80, *Wenwu* (1986.6), 89 and 95, *Kaogu* (1984.7), p. 669, *Kaogu* (1987.10), 890-8. A mirror similar to the square piece in Plate 81 has been published by Dr Pak as Korean, Pak p. 50. She does refer to a similar Song mirror inscribed as made in Hangzhou.

131 See: *Wenwu* (1956.9), p. 76, *Wenwu* (1957.8), p. 31, *Wenwu* (1958.6), p. 63, *Wenwu* (1959.10), p. 85. Yuen Ting Chuek, 'A Study of Hu Chou Mirrors in Southern Sung Dynasty', *The Journal of the Institute of Chinese Studies of the*

Chinese University of Hong Kong, XVII (1986), 145–62.

132 *Zhejiang chutu tong jing* ('Excavated Bronze Mirrors from Zhejiang Province'), edited by Wang Shilun (Beijing, 1987), 21–3, pls. 182, 183, 185.

133 A mirror signed Xue Jinhou is illustrated in *Wenwu* (1986.7), p. 88, where it is attributed to the Song dynasty; the piece is not excavated.

134 Sample spectra produced by Gretchen Shearer using diffuse reflectance methods, on a Perkin-Elmer 1700 Infrared Fourier Transform Spectrometer.

135 An identical mirror is illustrated in Milan Rupert and O. J. Todd, *Chinese Bronze Mirrors: A study based on the Todd Collection of 1,000 bronze mirrors found in the five northern provinces of Suiyuan, Shensi, Shansi, Honan and Hopei, China* (Peking, 1935), no. 352, p. 225, pl. XXIX.

136 Chen Baiquan, 'Ji Yuan Ming shiqi Jiangxi zhuzao de tongjing' ('Some Yuan and Ming dynasty bronze mirrors from Jiangxi province'), *Kaogu* (1988.7), 636–7.

137 The composition was a 'group A' alloy (see note 126).

138 One of them is illustrated in *Ku Kung t'ung ching hsuan ts'ui* (Masterpieces of Chinese Bronze Mirrors in the National Palace Museum), (Taipei, 1971), pl. 50.

139 *Xi Qing gu jian, juan* 40, p. 35.

140 Wen, *juan* 7, p. 274.

141 A similar piece in the Palace Museum in Peking is illustrated in *Gugong bowuyuan yuankan* (1984.2), pl. 7. The *xiniu* is generally depicted gazing back up at the moon over its shoulder, following the theme of a popular story. It is a common decoration on ceramics and mirrors during the Song and Yuan periods (see Plate 89).

142 A similiar scene is shown on Song and Jin mirrors in *Kaogu yu wenwu* (1982.3), p. 102 and *Wenwu* (1984.2), p. 79, while a Yuan example with identical wave-pattern is shown in *Wenwu* (1979.8), p. 35.

Select Bibliography

Bureau of Cultural Properties, *Relics from the Seabed at Sinan* (Seoul, 1983)

R. Soame Jenyns and William Watson, *Chinese Art: The Minor Arts, Volume 1* (London, 1965 and Oxford, 1981)

Rose Kerr, 'The Evolution of Bronze Style in the Jin, Yuan and Early Ming Dynasties', *Oriental Art*, 28 (1982.2), 146-58

Rose Kerr, 'Metalwork and Song Design: A Bronze Vase Inscribed in 1173', *Oriental Art*, 32 (1986.2), 161-76

Hugo Munsterberg, *Chinese Buddhist Bronzes* (New York, 1988)

National Palace Museum, *Ku Kung t'ung ching hsuan ts'ui (Masterpieces of Chinese Bronze Mirrors in the National Palace Museum)*, (Taipei, 1971)

Jessica Rawson, *Ancient China, Art and Archaeology* (London, 1980)

William Watson, 'On Some Categories of Archaism in Chinese Bronze', *Ars Orientalis*, 9 (1973), 3-13.

Index

References in **bold type** are Plate numbers, not pages.